The Old Rectory
Whitchurch
Shropshire

To Valerie
with love from
Jean.

APRIL 2007

The Old Rectory Whitchurch Shropshire

by

Jean North
Madge Moran
Joan Barton

Logaston Press

LOGASTON PRESS
Little Logaston Woonton Almeley
Herefordshire HR3 6QH
logastonpress.co.uk

First published by Logaston Press 2007
Copyright © Jean North, Madge Moran & Joan Barton 2007

ISBN 978 1904396 69 7

Set in Times by Logaston Press
and printed in Great Britain by
The Cromwell Press, Trowbridge

This book is dedicated to

DAVID AND GRACE JENKINS

*in appreciation of their work for the people of Whitchurch
and especially for David's ministry there from 1973 to 1997*

Contents

Acknowledgements   *ix*

A Note on the Rector's Books   *x*

Introduction   *xi*

1 The Early History and Background   1

2 The Middle Years   5

3 The Eighteenth Century   11

4 An Erratic Divine   21

5 The Nineteenth Century   33

6 The Twentieth Century   43

7 Rectors of Whitchurch   49

8 Wartime at the Old Rectory: The 'Y' Station   63

Appendix   89

Glossary   91

References   93

Index   99

Acknowledgements

We acknowledge with thanks the assistance given to us by many people: George Baugh for detailed and time-consuming help with the history, particularly that relating to the Rectors, North Shropshire District Council for help with accessing the site, the staff at Shropshire Archives and the Reference Library in Shrewsbury and the staff at the Caldicott Library in Whitchurch. Mrs. M. Jones-Owen kindly loaned the lithograph printed in 1797 and allowed us to copy it and we are also grateful to Mr. Tom Biggins of Westry Roberts, Pauline Stokes, a former verger, and to Margaret O'Neill, the present owner of 'Highfields'. The section on the rôle of the Old Rectory during World War Two as a 'Y' station took much researching. Jean and Stanley North had an early suspicion that it was being used for secret wireless telegraphy, but it was not until this was confirmed by Bletchley Park that progress could be made. Stanley's sad death in 2001 meant that Jean had to continue the research on her own and for help with this we are particularly grateful to Mr. David White of the diplomatic wireless service at Bletchley Park. Tracking down wireless operators who worked at the Old Rectory resulted in valuable information from Mrs. J. Briggs, Mrs. M. Rudd, Mrs. J. Broadhurst, Mrs. B. Griffiths, Mrs. E. Allen and particularly from Mrs. B. Hayes. We extend thanks to all these and to the naval staff including Mr. E. Mead and Mr. G. Rudd and the post-war intake of Mr. J. Evans and Mr. H. Travers. Mr. B. Lowry of the 'Defence of Britain' project took a great interest in our work and put us on the trail of the Ministry of Works documents in the archives for which we are grateful. Similarly Mark Baldwin of the Enigma Bulletin guided our searches and allowed us to photograph the Enigma machine in his possession. Peter Howell took many of our old slides and turned them into usable prints. Those who helped with the supply of old photographs are acknowledged in the captions and Mr. W. Moran is thanked for most of the recent ones. Once again we thank the Owen Family Trust for the financial support which has enabled us to publish our work, and we thank Andy Johnson of Logaston Press for his patience, skills and publishing expertise without which our efforts would have been in vain.

In 1997 the class which was at that time sponsored by Keele University's Department of Adult and Continuing Education comprised: Patricia Gates, Judith Hoyle, Kathleen Priddy, Joan Barton, June Potter, Janet Miller, Jean North, Stanley North, Mary Perry, Richard Hughes, Stuart Finch, Grace Jenkins, Barbara Latham and Madge Moran (Tutor).

Each member helped either with the measuring or with the historical research, and Dr. Judith Hoyle's expertise with computers was particularly valuable. Pat Gates' expertise with staircase drawings started the recording programme and Jean North was responsible for all the presentation drawings.

Our debt to David and Grace Jenkins is immense. They have encouraged and helped us in so many ways, and it is with great pleasure that we dedicate this work to them.

A note on the 'Rector's Books'

Much of the material in this present work is based on the 'Rector's Books'. These are two large bound volumes which are kept in the Vestry of the parish church, St. Alkmund's Whitchurch. They contain a miscellany of papers relating to the church, the rectory and various matters affecting the parish and the district. The collection was assembled by the Rev. Francis Henry Egerton who became rector in 1781 and he bequeathed it to his successors 'for ever'. He died in 1829, but the last dated item is notification of a Visitation dated 12 June 1857, suggesting that at least one or two of the subsequent incumbents added to the accumulation, though half-heartedly.

To call the books 'scrap-books' would be misleading. It is true that they have that quality, but consisting as they do of original plans, petitions, tithes, correspondence, poor relief, schools both in Whitchurch and Wem and much more they are an invaluable record and a source of primary material for the modern historian. For architectural historians the collection is particularly valuable as it contains drawings by well-known architects not to be found in any national archive.

When the Rev. David Jenkins became rector in 1973 he found the books in a very dilapidated state, completely unusable. Aware of their potential and historic value he and his wife, Grace, arranged for the Owen Family Trust (of which Grace is a trustee) to pay for them to be properly restored, put in order and rebound. Some of the documents are missing, and the index which was made after the books were restored cannot be relied upon. Researchers may have access to the books by appointment with either the present rector or the verger.

Our grateful thanks are extended to David and Grace and to the present rector, Andrew Ridley, for permission to use the books. Without them our work would be much poorer. The drawings in the books are impossible to photo-copy, and indeed would suffer from the attempt, so Jean North has painstakingly traced those that we considered the most interesting and relevant, reluctantly omitting many of arguably lesser worth, and has added many of her own drawings done recently. Proposed alterations on the original drawings are mostly shown in colour, either pink or yellow, and so Jean has used the convention of dots or hatching on her tracings. Most of the documents are in their original hand, but some — especially the drawings — have clearly been captioned later and should, therefore, be used with caution. Although an attempt has been made to put the papers into chronological order this may not be correct in all cases and again caution is advised.

Plate 2 The 'Rector's Books'

Introduction

The Old Rectory at Whitchurch (SJ 542420) is located less than ¼ mile to the north of the parish church. At present it seems to be isolated from it, but this is because an early Whitchurch by-pass to the east of the town is routed between the two (fig. 1). The house itself stands in an isolated position and is approached down a lane, at present unnamed, but which is shown on some of the old maps as Love Lane, off Claypit Street. It has been unused for many years, has suffered neglect and opportunist disposal of land and is included in North Shropshire's Conservation Department's 'Buildings at Risk' register although listed as a Grade II. The Whitchurch Buildings Recording Group, at the time an extramural class sponsored by Keele University, first saw the building in 1997 and did some preliminary measuring then, but did not have the chance to finish the project. However, in the meantime, North Shropshire District Council's Planning Department ensured that the building was, at least, made safe, and in 2003 the class was able to resume work, although it was still not possible to have access to all parts. What emerged was the recognition of a very old

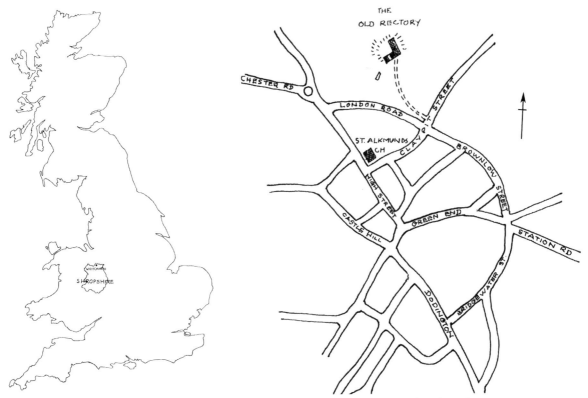

Figure 1 Location plans for the Old Rectory, Whitchurch

historic site, an eighteenth-century rectory of quality built with style in the fashion of the time, a comfortable family home for people of means and, during the Second World War, a vital link in the secret code-breaking system between Bletchley Park in Buckinghamshire and scattered receiving stations. Thus, the Old Rectory at Whitchurch, a 'Y' station, played a part in the amazing 'Enigma' saga. Some would say that this was its 'finest hour'.

1   THE EARLY HISTORY & BACKGROUND

In the Domesday Book (1086) the site later to become 'Whitchurch' is referred to as Westune ('west settlement') and the surrounding hamlets also have Saxon names, for example Alkington, Dodington, Edgeley, Hinton and Tilstock.[1] The dedication to the church to St. Alkmund is also significant as is the tradition that the first church was founded by Ethelfleda, the lady of the Mercians in *c.*912 AD.[2] The 1880 O.S. map of Whitchurch marks the site of the old Rectory as 'Site of Monastery' and shows it surrounded on three sides by a moat (fig. 2). Part of this moat survives (pl. 3) and heavy rains still fill it to some extent. However, there are no known records

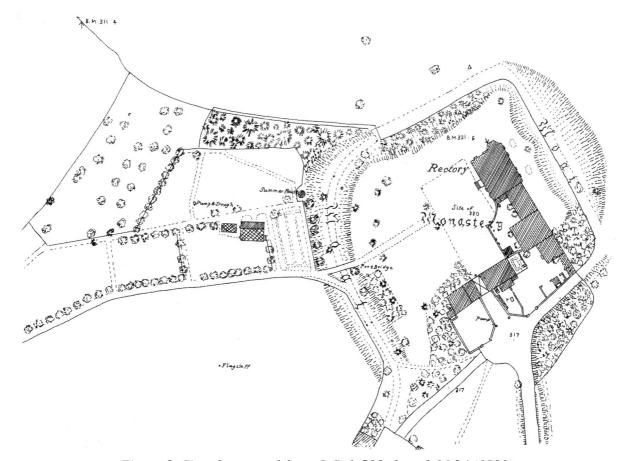

Figure 2 Site plan traced from O.S. 1:500 sheet 1.16.24 (1880)

Plate 3 Remains of the Moat

of any monastic activity in the area and it is more likely that what is meant is a dwelling of clergy serving the Minster church of Westune, the centre of the 'parochia', which had a college of priests serving the area before the present parish came into existence.

The early dedication of the church, the probability of multiple priests, the named dependent hamlets and the land attached to the church taken together strongly imply Minster status. The church itself was not taxable and held no land in its own right — it was considered to belong to God — so the lack of mention in Domesday does not imply that there was no church in Whitchurch at that time. It is therefore feasible that the site of the old Rectory has been occupied by clergy since the time of Ethelfleda. Certainly, much uncertainty surrounds the early history of the site. It has been suggested that it was that of a monastic hospital[3] or, alternatively, the site of the early manor house belonging to the le Strange family.[4] But neither of these can be sustained. From very early times the manor house of Whitchurch was located at Blakemere, just over a mile to the north-east, and Fulk le Strange, who died in 1324, held the manor from Earl William Warenne 'by service of taking the venison throughout the Earl's lands.'[5] Earl William was keeper of the castle in Whitchurch and his daughter Alianore married Robert le Strange. Fulk was their son, born in 1289, and it was he who obtained a 'licence to crennelate' his dwelling house (*mansum suum*) of Whitchurch.[6] In effect this probably meant that he rebuilt Blakemere, having re-united the manor after Earl William's other three daughters had been endowed. Certainly by the late thir-

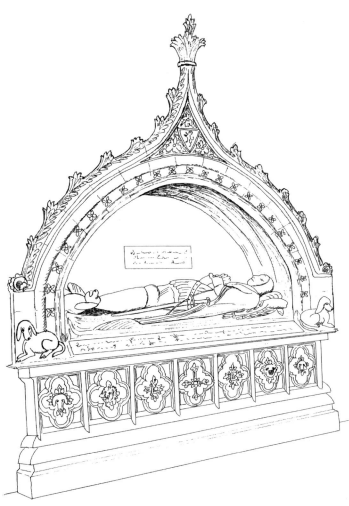

*Figure 3 Tomb of Lord John Talbot,
Earl of Shrewsbury*

teenth century the le Strange family was resident at Blakemere.[7] Fulk became the first Lord Strange of Blakemere and his eldest son, John, who succeeded in 1325, married Ankaret, daughter and co-heir of William Botiller of Wem.[8] Ankaret features in the history of the Old Rectory, as will be seen later, and one of her descendants, another Ankaret, was the mother of John Talbot, the legendary warrior depicted so graphically by Shakespeare in *Henry VI Part I* (fig. 3).

The advowson or patronage of Whitchurch, that is, the right to present the rector, belonged to the Warennes and their successors as lords of the manor. It was a valuable right, for the rectory was one of the richest parochial livings in Shropshire.[9]

The first recorded parson in Whitchurch was James Fraunceys who had a letter of protection in 1296/7 in the reign of Edward I. A non-resident parson called John de Knouvill was in office from 1310 to 1337 when, on 1 April, King Edward III confirmed Bartholomew de Berdefelde as Rector of Whitchurch. He also mentions 'the donation which Fulk le Strange de Albo Monasterie had made to God, to St. Mary, to St. Alkmund and to the Rectors of St. Alkmund of Albo Monasterium viz: a parcel of land called La Withians-leghe,[10] with a vivary adjacent thereto, to hold, as the said Bartholomew and his predecessors had held it before time'. Bartholomew died in 1358 and it was then that Robert le Strange was presented to the living by Dame Ankaret, Lady of Blakemere and Whitchurch, but their relationship is not known. It was she who later presented Roger de Thrisk to the living in 1409. It is recorded that Roger showed his gratitude by donating one cow to Lord Talbot's household.[11] In 1401–2, probably during his absence from Whitchurch, the rector, Thomas Welford, let his living to the patron, who, in return for a rent paid to the rector, received some £19 8s. 3d. that year and paid out £5 19s. 3d. on chaplains' stipends, ecclesiastical fees and dues (e.g. Peter's Pence), repairs to the rector's tithe barn and dovecot, and charges for carting tithe grain from outlying parts of the parish to Whitchurch.[12] The arrangement probably indicates good relations between rector and patron, the rector receiving a competent rent from the lord, whom he trusted to look after his interests for the term of his absence.

'Album Monasterium' or 'Blancminster' were Norman names for the settlement later to become simply 'Whitchurch'. It has been assumed that the Norman church was built of white Grinshill stone, hence the derivation, but this is unlikely. The quarries at Grinshill were not exploited until later in medieval times and the distance of over twenty miles to transport the stone would be a drawback. The most likely explanation is that the church was rendered and white-washed, as were many important buildings in early days.

The land surrounding the Old Rectory is low lying and winter rains often replenish the moat and various depressions, one of which in the field adjoining the London Road north of the church-yard is likely to be the site of the vivary, a very necessary source of food for the priest and his household who served the community before the Reformation. A copyhold surrender document of 1400 includes 'half a burgage in the said town between a burgage of Roger Ostag and the pond of the rector of the said town', confirming that the fishpond or vivary was still a feature.[13]

2 THE MIDDLE YEARS

Little is known about the Old Rectory in the fifteenth and sixteenth centuries, but some of the documents relating to the seventeenth century are helpful. A Terrier dated 14 October 1612 when Anthony Buckley was the minister describes a Parsonage house of seven bays with garden, dove house, gatehouse of three bays and a barn of three bays all within the moat, and outside the moat were a kiln of two bays and a seven-bayed barn. Several pieces of land and messuages are also included.[1] With minor variations this form prevailed over the succeeding years and an inventory of the rector, Matthew Fowler (1666–1683), transcribed in the Appendix, gives an image of the house later in the seventeenth century. He had six bedchambers, a great and a little parlour, a hall and a kitchen as well as a coach-house and stables for four horses, farming implements and brewing vessels. By far the largest item, £700, is his 'Bills, bonds and debts', showing not only his considerable personal wealth but his function as the local unofficial banker, lending money at interest. The item, 'A pair of Harpsnalls', perhaps emphasizes his comfortable living. 'Harpsnalls' is a harpsichord, pluralized because there were two keyboards.[2] The fact that the appraisers arrived at the wrong total is not unusual, especially with those involving large sums. Clearly the rector had an enviable lifestyle and was able to augment his income by farming. Though virtually rebuilt, the tithe barn in which the tithes paid by his parishioners were stored still remains and is currently in use as a cheese storage warehouse by Messrs Westry Roberts & Co. As a mark of historic respect the roof structure of the industrial part of the warehouse was copied from that which was found there, and this, it is thought, is the king-post roof depicted on fig. 4. Though not dated, it is likely to have part of the rebuilding programme of 1749. The timber-framed and brick building opposite the tithe barn was probably converted to a coach-house

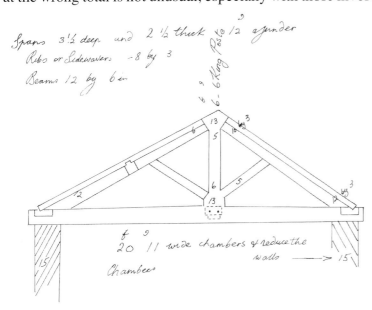

Figure 4 King-post roof believed to have existed at the tithe barn (traced from the Rector's Books)

Plate 4 The Tithe Barn (left) and Coach House as depicted by Denise Rylands

at the same time, the brickwork being virtually identical with that of the house. A painting by Denise Rylands (pl. 4) depicts these two buildings as they were before modern conversion.[3] The Hearth Tax return for 1662 (Michaelmas) records that Dr. Fowler's predecessor, Richard Heylin D.D. paid sixteen shillings on the eight hearths in the house.[4]

A Terrier made a few years later in 1701 states that 'The Parsonage House consists of seven small bays of building, the Gatehouse and two bays adjoining, the Dove House, the stable, four small bays. One large shed adjoining to the house next the stable. Another large shed with a stable adjoining to it. Two Privys, the Parsonage Court containing two perches of land, the Dovehouse garden, nineteen perches, the little garden, three perches, the stable fold, fourteen perches, Noal Gate[5] [*sic*], two perches, the great garden, one pole, thirty-one perches. The garden by the privy, two perches, all moated round'. Other items included the Kiln of three small bays, the Parsonage barn of seven small bays, five other houses on glebe land, the bridge and meadows, the Stew and Stew Croft, the school croft and the school hole.[6] Again, a picture emerges of a comparatively rich living enjoyed by an almost self-sufficient rector (Clement Sankey D.D.) and his household. Seven bays, however 'small', were generous, and the building would compare, perhaps, with the size and appearance of the old Raven Inn in Watergate, Whitchurch, which has been dendro-dated to 1625.[7] That had six bays, but three of those measured sixteen feet each. However, the parsonage had the advantage of a two-bayed gatehouse in addition to the house. The incumbent cannot have been short of accommodation.

6

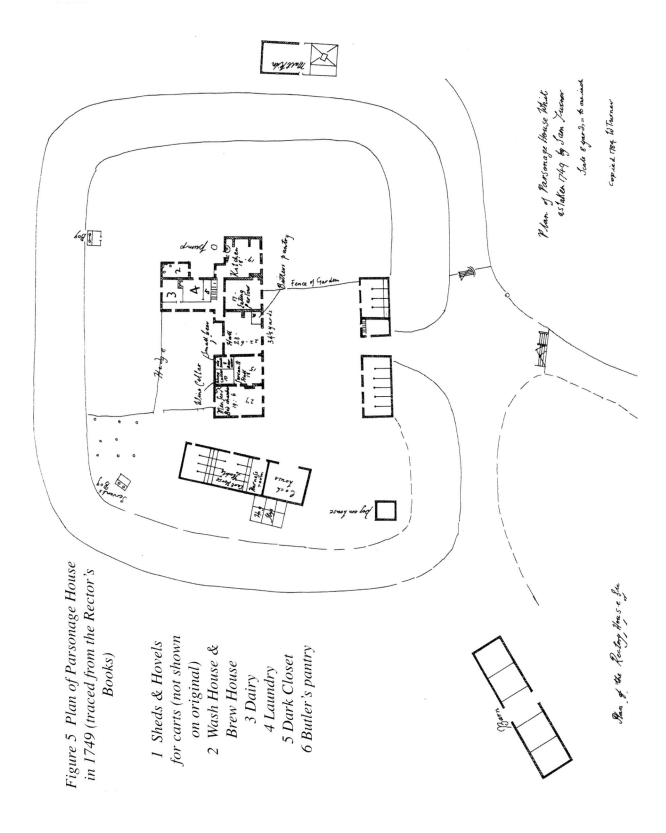

Figure 5 Plan of Parsonage House in 1749 (traced from the Rector's Books)

1 Sheds & Hovels for carts (not shown on original)
2 Wash House & Brew House
3 Dairy
4 Laundry
5 Dark Closet
6 Butler's pantry

7

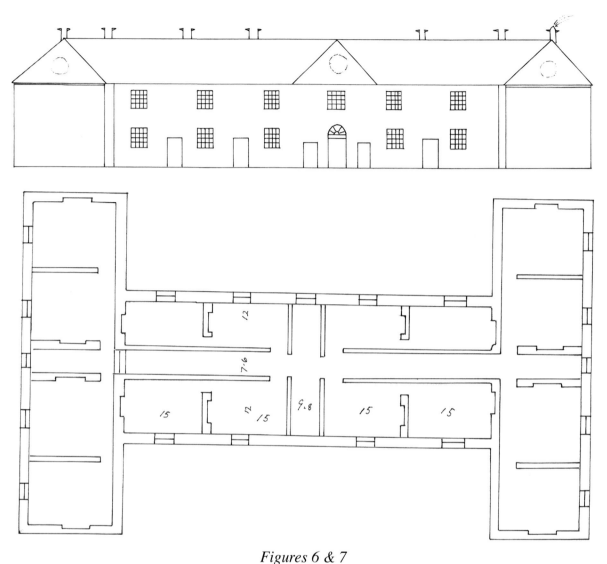

Figures 6 & 7
Plan and elevation of the Rectory before it was pulled down by Dr. Newcome,
Bishop of St. Asaph (but thought to be wrongly captioned) (traced from the Rector's Books)

There is a small possibility that Sankey's house may have been altered towards the end of the century because a drawing of the site plan made by the Whitchurch architect, Samuel Turner, prior to its demolition in 1749 shows a five-bayed house (fig. 5). Even an allowance for the hall to be of two bays would only result in six bays for the house, but there may have been an element of carelessness in the Terrier. The Rector's Book I contains other drawings which purport to be the elevation and plan of the rectory before it was pulled down (figs. 6 & 7). Even by earlier standards these are not of good quality and it is difficult to reconcile them with Turner's plan. Neither is signed and they each show an H-shaped building of five bays with projecting cross-wings at either end. The three gables (two at either end and the central pediment) each contain a circular window and the whole frontage is entirely symmetrical. Six chimneys are shown and the windows

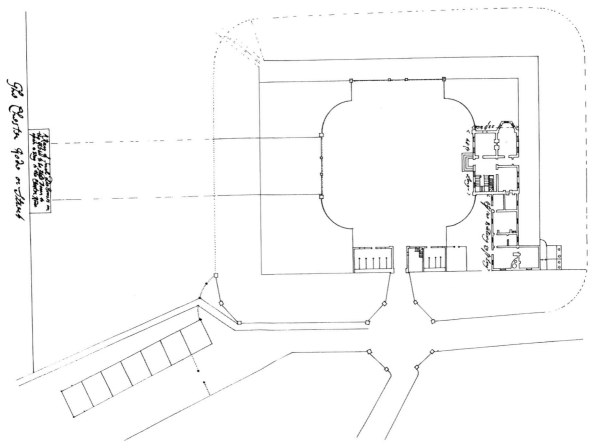

Figure 8 'A Rang of Small olde Houses On the Glebe to be pul'd down to open a Way to the Chester Rode', *as shown on a drawing dated 1749 (traced from the Rector's Books)*

appear to be standard eighteenth-century sashes. No timbering is shown, the main door is centrally placed, and, curiously, four additional doors appear on the front. It is suggested that these drawings relate to a different building entirely and have been wrongly captioned. It is perhaps more likely that they illustrate the range of 'old decayed houses standing on the glebe adjoining to the turnpike road from Whitchurch to Chester' which, according to the Faculty for the rebuilding of the rectory, were to be demolished. The symmetrical division of the rooms and the longitudinal central corridor suggest an institutional use of some kind.[8] They appear as a block on the Faculty plan for rebuilding in 1749 where they are labelled '*A Rang of Small olde Houses On the Glebe to be pul'd down to open a Way to the Chester Rode*' (fig. 8). On this it is clear that when the rectory was rebuilt on a new alignment a wide driveway was intended to lead straight from the Chester road to the front door of the house, but this was never implemented. The plan also shows the seven-bayed Parsonage barn mentioned in the 1701 Terrier.

On Turner's plan the frontage of the rectory is given as '34½ yds'. If the basic bay is taken as sixteen feet this gives a building of just over six full-sized bays with a hall of two bays, clearly the most important room in the house. The plan has most of the parts labelled, and, in addition to the hall, these include a servants' hall, wine cellar, butler's pantry, eating parlour, kitchen and men servants' bed chamber. A service range to the rear contains a dairy, laundry, wash-house, brew-house and a 'dark closet' while a large farming block with a coach-house, harness room and cart-house is located to the west. This block has pig-sties to the rear. Also within the moated area are a pigeon house and two two-seater 'bogs', one for the servants, the other, presumably, for the family. The gate-house at the entrance appears to be serving as stables at this time, although it is not labelled as such. There seems to be stabling for ten horses. The only buildings outside the moat are a barn in the south-west corner and a malt-kiln to the east. The moat is clearly defined and the entrance is gated as is the approach to the malt-kiln.

3 THE EIGHTEENTH CENTURY

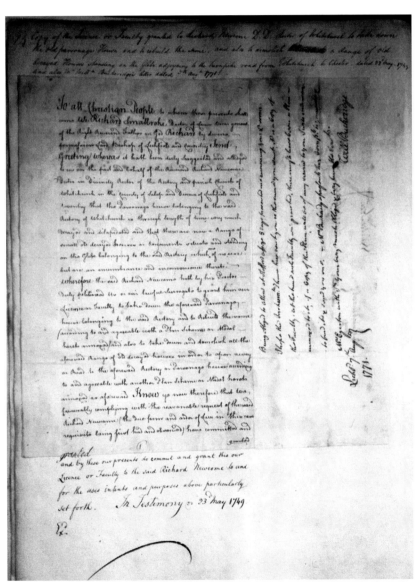

*Plate 5 Copy of the faculty for the demolition
of the pre-1749 Rectory*

The house described in the previous chapter was demolished in 1749 following the granting of a faculty allowing a new one to be built (pl. 5).[1] The incumbent at the time was a Dr. Newcome who was also a canon of Windsor and a future bishop of Llandaff and St. Asaph. The 1749 date seems to be well supported by the documentary evidence although it should be noted that a later Terrier of 1756 gives that year for the rebuilding and another of 1884 gives the date of the rebuilding as 1760.[2] A Terrier made on 23 July 1849 gives the information that the old Terriers stated that the parsonage lands contained 29 acres, 1 rood and 11 perches but that a recent survey gave 35 acres, 17 roods. It records 'A Parsonage House built of brick and slated, with outbuildings, glebe lands and gardens adjoining'.[3] This is the house which stands at present and it is interesting to compare it with what is known of its predecessor. The old house

Plate 6 The gate-house in 2005

was approached directly from the gate-house, as was normal, but the new one took no account of the old siting and was aligned to the east on a north-west — south-east axis, though still within the moated area.

THE OLD RECTORY AT PRESENT

As will be seen later, various suggestions were made to 'improve' the house built in 1749 or thereabouts but, perhaps fortunately, most of them came to nothing and the house as it stands is basically that which was built for Dr. Newcome. The unknown quantity is the name of the architect. It is reasonable to suggest that it was Samuel Turner as he made the site plan recording the lay-out prior to demolition of the existing house in 1749, but there is nothing in the Terriers, the Rector's Books or any available documentation to confirm or deny that he was responsible for its replacement, whilst there is evidence, discussed below, that Thomas Farnolls Pritchard, a better-known Shropshire architect, was involved. Turner was a local man, one of a family of architects based in Whitchurch whose various members were employed in country houses, churches and other public buildings in Shropshire and the surrounding counties. Clearly the family firm was well thought of and Samuel was commended for his 'honest dealing' when he was employed at Hawarden Castle.[4]

Although the new house was aligned differently, it was still inwardly facing instead of looking out over the open countryside, but in some other respects it represents what has come to be called the 'Age of Enlightenment' when classic design prevailed and common sense dictated simple rectangular shapes for outline, entrance doors and sash windows. 'Simplified Georgian Classic' would aptly describe the architecture of the Old Rectory.

The West (front) Elevation (fig. 9 and pl. 6))

Five bays wide and two-and-a half stories high, the house is brick-built in Flemish bond. The gable walls accommodate the two end chimneystacks and are finished with coping stones, but there are no kneelers. Instead, the coping stones are brought out to form the top course of a brick parapet which rises from a plain cornice of Grinshill stone. The parapet conceals three dormer windows which light the attic space. Each of the main windows is a twelve-light recessed sash, has a window-sill of Grinshill stone and brick voussoirs set as a plain lintel with no pronounced keystone. The main entrance doorway is centrally placed and has a triangular pediment above a plain entablature. The doorway is flanked by two attached columns in the Doric order and is approached by a short flight of shallow steps. Level with the top step is a slightly projecting brick

Figure 9 and Plate 6 The West Elevation

13

plinth below which the tops of the cellar windows are visible. These have similar voussoirs, but the glazing has been largely destroyed. From the remains they seem to have had smaller panes of sixteen lights each. Clearly the cellars were well-lit.

The East (rear) Elevation (fig. 10)
Originally the rear elevation would have mirrored the front, and, as shown on the Faculty drawing (fig. 8) there was a rear entrance opposite the front door. At present there is no evidence of a rear doorway unless it could be argued that the brickwork below the present window is slightly different from the remainder. The secondary entrance is currently located on the south side. A striking feature of the rear elevation at present is the row of brick buttresses, six half-height and four full-height which flank the ground-floor windows. These were necessary additions when the house was in use as a 'Y-station' during the Second World War. Also from this time date the mutilations of the windows themselves to make provision for the cables from the aerials to connect with the receivers (see later).

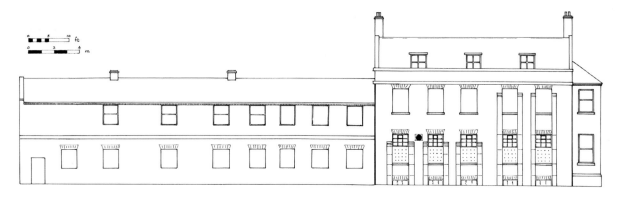

Figure 10 The East Elevation

The Plans (figs. 11, 12)
Basically the plan of the Old Rectory is very simple, with four main rooms on the ground floor matched by similar divisions above. On the first projected plan (fig. 13) a through passage from front to back is shown with a heated reception room, eighteen feet square, partitioned off on the right and the staircase given its own area at the back, but on the Faculty plan (fig. 8) the staircase is shown in its present position and, again as now, there is no fireplace. It could be argued that the original plan as on the Faculty and which largely applies at present would enable the house to be run more efficiently, but perhaps that is a matter for personal opinions. The staircase is certainly an impressive feature and is discussed more fully below. The other rooms at ground level were a small morning room or parlour and a dining room/library. The latter has a distinctive canted bay window which is repeated in the room above. This is not necessarily a later addition although it has a Victorian ambience. It is shown on three drawings in the Rector's Book I which purport to depict the house 'as built by the Bishop of St. Asaph' who was, in fact, Richard Newcombe[5] (figs. 13, 14, 15). Unfortunately none is dated and the name of the architect is not given. A further drawing (fig. 16) is not captioned. Figs. 13 and 14 and 16 show elevations with differences in the treatment

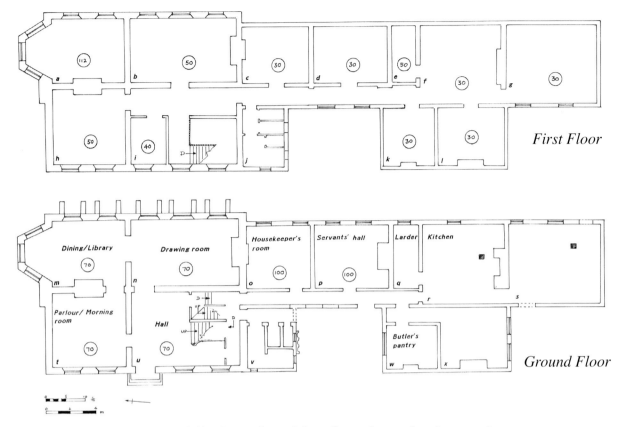

First Floor

Ground Floor

Figures 11 and 12 Ground- and first-floor plans, showing wartime use
First Floor*: a) Set room for high speed Morse; PBX switchboard; floor strengthened*
b) Engineers' room   c) Rest room   d, e, f, g) Additional set rooms; f & g were strengthened
by piers below   h) Typing room; Undulator tapes read and typed for collection by Station X
(Bletchley Park)   i) Engineers' room   j) Ladies' lavatories (1941-2)
k & l) Administration offices

Ground Floor*: m) Set room with 6 HRO receivers; high-speed Morse*
n) Set room with 6 HRO receivers; supervisor's desk; aerial amplifiers and distribution panel
o) secure teleprinter links to HQ   p) Set room with 4-6 receivers in high-speed Morse on undu-
lator tape   q) Original larder   r & s) 13½ x 13½ brick piers in tile-finished floors (1942);
r was the original kitchen, known as the 'Baronial Hall' by 'Y' staff; s was there before 1880;
t) Main set room with internal switchboard   u) Contained notice boards and duty rosters
v) Previous bathroom converted to men's lavatory in 1941–2; v was there before 1880; urinals
shown on outer wall were covered with a cast-iron roof
w) Original butler's pantry converted to men's lavatory in 1941–2; w & x were there before 1880
Note*: The plans are drawn as in 2004 but with approximate measurements in the service wing*
as no access was possible. The lay-out of the receivers and other equipment is largely based on
the memories of personnel that we have been able to contact and additional details are taken
from the Ministry of Works plans 1941–2 showing the addition of the lavatories and urinals. The
superloads are given in lbs per sq. ft and circled. (SA 3244/1-3).

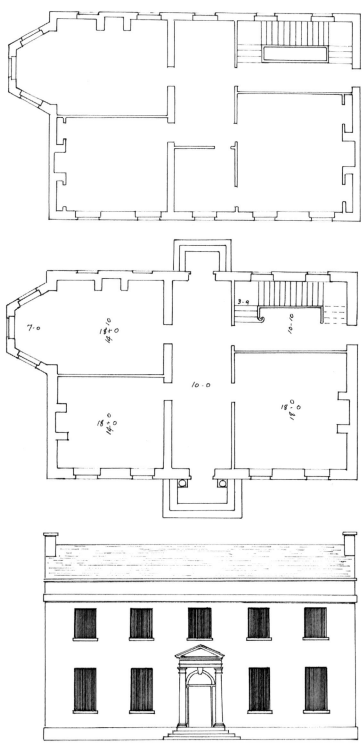

*Figure 13 Projected front elevation and ground-floor plan
(centre) and chamber floor (top) of the Rectory
(traced from the Rector's Books)*

of the main block and figs. 14 and 16 show major differences in the service wing. As it exists today the main block is an amalgam of 14 and 16 but the service block is totally different.

The crucial question is whether or not the original plan was implemented. On the whole it seems that it was. The rear door is shown on later plans and there is little evidence to show that the staircase position was ever moved. The only slight anomaly is on the face of the wall which forms the left boundary of the staircase. Here the cornice moulding stops short of the return, but, of course, other factors could account for this.

Service Rooms

The lay-out of the rooms described above does not take into account the rooms which would be required to service a household such as that of the parson of a rich living. It is difficult to reconcile the drawings in the Rector's Book I, mentioned above, with the situation that prevails particularly as access to these rooms was not possible. Measurements on the present drawings are, therefore, estimations and the use of the different rooms is suggested from various sources such as reminiscences from local people, 'Y-station' staff who worked there and from the Ministry of Works plans, 1941 and 1942.[6] Absolute necessities at ground level would be a kitchen, a servants' hall, a housekeeper's room, a butler's pantry and

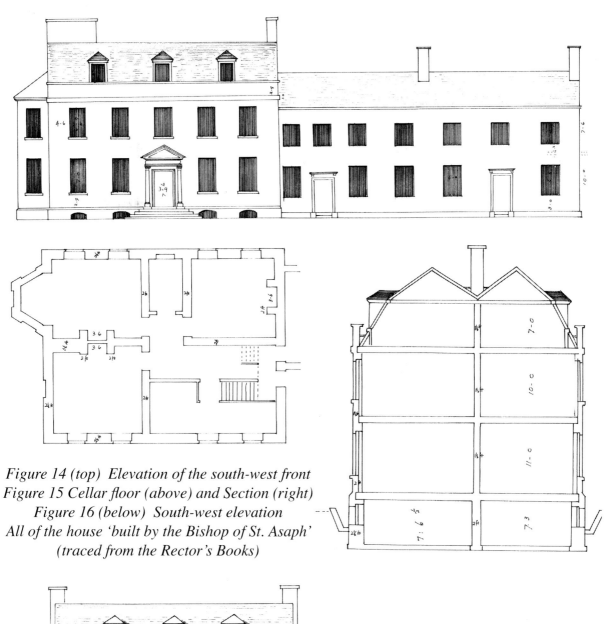

Figure 14 (top) Elevation of the south-west front
Figure 15 Cellar floor (above) and Section (right)
Figure 16 (below) South-west elevation
All of the house 'built by the Bishop of St. Asaph'
(traced from the Rector's Books)

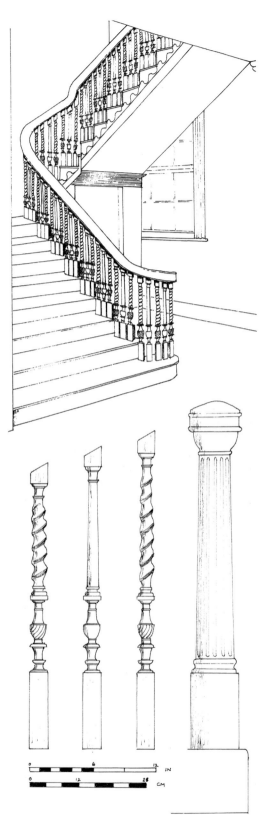

storage of some kind, although the cellars would have provided ample storage facilities. The bulk of these rooms were located in a line running south from the side of the main block, but the butler's pantry seems to have occupied a space at the front of the site, separated from the main block by some thirty-three feet. To reach the dining room the butler would have had to traverse a long corridor, negotiate various steps and enter through the hall (fig. 12). Nurseries and nannies' rooms were, presumably, located at first-floor level above the service rooms.

At some time it was found necessary to add to the service accommodation. Clearly the adjunct to the south-west corner of the main block, converted from a bathroom to a men's lavatory in wartime, comes into this category as does the end room of the eastward-running block. (See 'Key' for details of wartime use.)

Overall, the service provision occupied more space than the main living accommodation, but that, perhaps, is a reflection on the spirit of the age.

Figure 17 Details of staircase, balusters and newel post (left) at the Old Rectory
Above: Ceiling rose in Morning Room

18

The Staircase (fig. 17)

Very few original features of merit remain in the house, but an exception is the staircase which rises from the hall. Whitchurch has a reputation for good staircases and the example at the Old Rectory comes firmly within that genre. Perhaps that is why it was considered desirable to make it fully visible on entry to the hall and not to conceal it within its own area as shown on fig. 13. Classed as a 'Quarter-turn with winders'[7] and typical of its time in the mid-eighteenth century, it has three balusters to each tread and no string. As shown in the detailed drawings each tread supports two moulded and twisted balusters on either side of a moulded and turned one. But this only applies to the rising section. The balusters run the length of the landing upstairs and here the twisted and turned ones alternate. The hand-rail is comparatively plain, though moulded at the edges, and twists round at the bottom to accommodate the newel post, also shown in detail on the drawings. The newel post is in the form of a column, tapered, moulded and fluted. There are no pendants or finials and the tread-ends are shaped but not carved. The edge of the landing itself is moulded and it is thought that the soffits of the upper flight would have been plastered and moulded, but this has been vandalised.

Almost a 'carbon copy' of the staircase exists at High Hatton Hall in the parish of Stanton-upon-Hine Heath, about sixteen miles to the south-east of Whitchurch (fig. 18). Details of each staircase are shown on the drawings and while there is a slight varia-

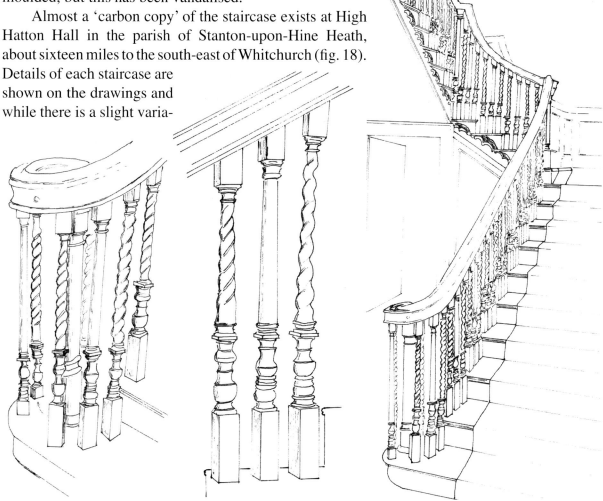

Figure 18 Sketches of the staircase at High Hatton hall, Stanton-upon-Hine Heath

tion in the form of the balusters and the newel posts and the rise is in opposite directions, almost certainly they were fashioned in the same architectural practice. Another very similar staircase is reported at High Wood, Bircher, in Herefordshire, part of the Croft Castle estate.[8] Croft Castle and High Hatton Hall are known to have been the work of the notable Shrewsbury architect, Thomas Farnolls Pritchard (1723–1777) who designed the world-famous first cast-iron bridge at Ironbridge.[9] This raises the question of whether Pritchard and not Turner was responsible for the whole design of the Old Rectory. One drawing, not in the Rector's Books and not signed by an architect, is included in documents relating to the Old Rectory (fig. 19).[10] It shows a Pritchardian-type double-storied three-canted bay window in plan and elevation with two detailed drawing below. On either side of the latter are outlines of classical cornice mouldings. All the features are beautifully drawn and the paper is captioned 'Window at General Egerton's'. This raises three questions: who was 'General' Egerton, was the title a mistake and is this Pritchard's work? These and other points will be discussed later.

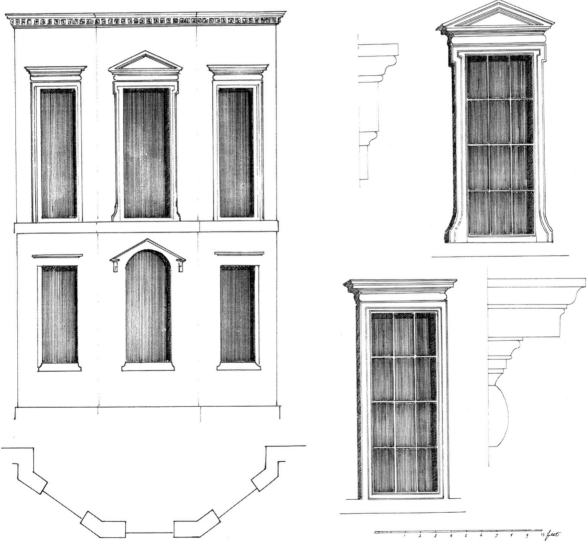

Figure 19 'Window at Gen. Egerton's' (traced from the Rector's Books)

20

4   AN ERRATIC DIVINE

For fifty years (1779–1829) the Rectory built in 1749 was home to Whitchurch's most eccentric yet beneficent rector, the Reverend Francis Henry Egerton, younger son of John Egerton, bishop of Durham. The main seat of the Egerton family was at Ashridge Park in Hertfordshire, but other lines of the family were seated in Cheshire at Tatton Park, Oulton Park, and Broxton Old Hall among other places. Francis Henry became rector of Whitchurch in 1781 when he was twenty-five years old and had the living of Myddle added in 1797, though when in Shropshire he lived in the Whitchurch rectory. Educated at Eton and Christ Church, Oxford, he was a man of intelligence, many talents and great wealth. He never married, so although, reputedly, he had five illegitimate daughters (pl. 8), the titles of Earl of Bridgwater, Viscount Brackley and Baron Ellesmere, was a Fellow of the Royal Society and a Fellow of the Society of Antiquaries of London, his line, title and lifestyle died with him in 1829.

Plate 8 Francis Henry Egerton and one of his alleged five illegitimate daughters

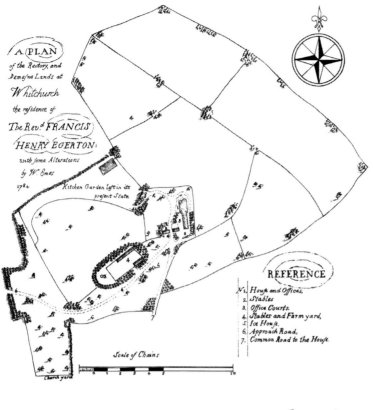

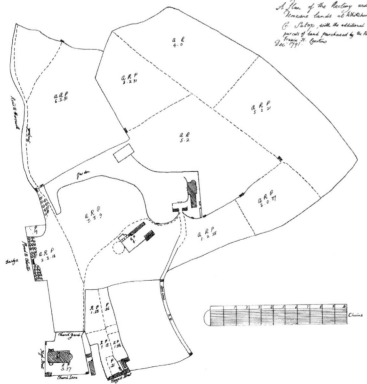

In many ways a typical eighteenth-century 'squarson', he enjoyed hunting and country pursuits, but he was also a fine scholar with a great love of literature. In his will he left land in the vicinity of the old Rectory to the Trustees of the British Museum and bequeathed his own manuscripts on the literature of France and Italy to them with an endowment of £7,000 for the augmentation of the collection. These are still known as the Egerton Manuscripts. He also left £8,000 to be paid to the author of the best treatise on the subject of 'The Goodness of God as manifested in the Creation' which was eventually awarded to eight authors of the 'Bridgwater Treatises' by the President of the Royal Society.[1]

He also left money to fund the building of the chapel at Tilstock, appropriately dedicated as Christ Church. This was built in 1835, six years after his death.[2]

In Whitchurch he is remembered for the bequest of his library, said to number some 2,000 books, for the use of the rector of Whitchurch forever. The same bequest included an endowment

Figure 20 (top) Plan showing William Emes' proposed alterations and improvements to the rectory
Figure 21 (bottom) Plan of 1791 showing the additional parcels of land bought by Francis Egerton (traced from the Rector's Books)

for the upkeep of the library from the sale of port wine in his cellar. Egerton's library was added to the great library left by Dr. Sankey (d.1707), originally bought by the Dowager Countess of Bridgwater, and given by her in 1717 to the church. In the mid 19th century W.H. Egerton, rector, thought that wider use of the books might be possible.[3]

In 1784 Mr. Egerton engaged William Emes to plan some alterations and improvements to the gardens at the rectory. Emes (1730–1803) was a landscape designer and gardener who favoured the style of Lancelot ('Capability') Brown and had worked at many of Shropshire's larger houses. He was also employed at Erddig in Denbighshire, the home of the Yorke family, and by the Brownlow family of Belton House in Lincolnshire. The three families were related.[4]

A plan showing Emes's proposals at the Rectory gives the impression that it was mostly shelter belts of trees that he had in mind, but he specifically noted that the kitchen garden to the north-west of the house was to be 'left in its present state'. Emes largely ignored the moat which by that time would have been redundant but could have been exploited as a garden or landscape feature[5] (fig. 20). At present it is difficult to assess how much of Emes's work survives, if, indeed his proposals were fully implemented, and the role of the Rectory in the Second World War as a 'Y' station must have necessitated much tree felling. This aspect of the house is discussed in a later chapter.

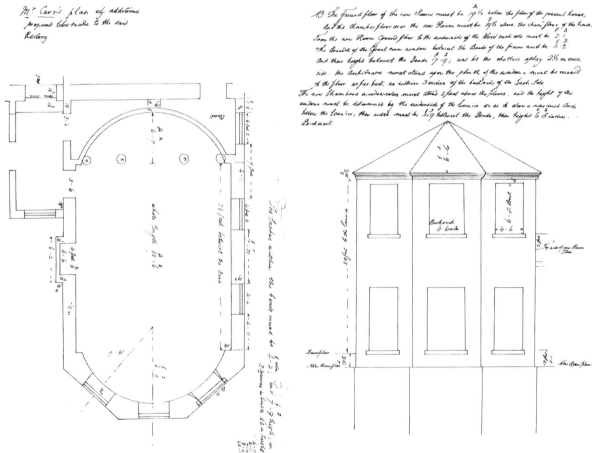

Figure 22 Mr. Carr's plan of proposed additions to the Rectory (traced from the Rector's Books)

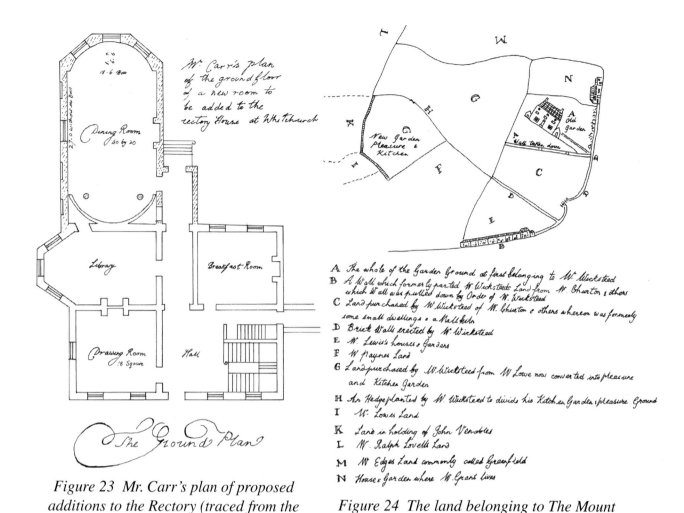

Mr Carr's plan of the ground floor of a new room to be added to the rectory House at Whitchurch

Dining Room 40 by 20

Library

Breakfast Room

Drawing Room 18 Square

Hall

The Ground Plan

A The whole of the Garden Ground at first belonging to Mr Wicksteed
B A Wall which formerly parted Mr Wicksteeds Land from Mr Churton & others which Wall was pulled down by Order of Mr Wicksteed
C Land purchased by Mr Wicksteed of Mr Churton & others whereon was formerly some small dwellings & a Malt kiln
D Brick Walls erected by Mr Wicksteed
E Mr Lewis's houses & Gardens
F Mr paynes Land
G Land purchased by Mr Wicksteed from Mr Lowe now converted into pleasure and Kitchen Garden
H An Hedge planted by Mr Wicksteed to divide his Kitchen Garden & pleasure Ground
I Mr Lowes Land
K Land in holding of John Venables
L Mr Ralph Lovells Land
M Mr Edges Land commonly called Greenfield
N House & Garden where Mr Grant lives

Figure 23 Mr. Carr's plan of proposed additions to the Rectory (traced from the Rector's Books)

Figure 24 The land belonging to The Mount (traced from the Rector's Books)

In 1791, or shortly before, Francis Henry Egerton was adding to his land holdings. These are shown in a map of the Demesne lands (fig. 21), and it is possible that he was also planning to extend the rectory at this time. Drawings by the architect Willey Reveley are contained in the Rector's Book 1 and these are dated to October 1789 and will be discussed below, but catalogued earlier in the book are drawings by a 'Mr. Carr' (figs. 22 & 23). This seems to be the first of many alterations considered for the house. The drawings are not dated and neither is the full name of the architect given. It seems that Mr. Carr envisaged a large dining room built out to the east beyond the library. It was to have a three-canted bay window similar to that on the library, but larger, and an apsed end where it adjoined the library. This apsed end is very similar to that shown on Reveley's no. 3 plans, but in a different position. Two or four ornamental pillars were to give emphasis to this end on Mr. Carr's plan. The drawings are very detailed and, interestingly, show the staircase with its present configurations and with a cross passage from the front door to a doorway in the rear wall, features which re-occur in the first of the Reveley drawings. To reach the new dining room Mr. Carr designed a covered way out from the rear door and the room would be entered from the left hand side. Speculation regarding Mr. Carr's identity is given below under 'Architectural Assessment'.

The rector's eccentricity is vividly portrayed in a lawsuit brought against him by William Wickstead, a barrister member of an old Whitchurch family who lived at 'The Mount' Chester Road, Whitchurch. Though not 'close' neighbours in modern terms, their lands adjoined. The two men had quarrelled, probably over tithes payable on the extended garden at The Mount. A plan exists of the house and gardens at The Mount showing the old garden and the newly-bought land which Mr. Wickstead was using for a pleasure and kitchen garden, and a note on the back records that only ancient gardens and orchards were liable for tithe payment (fig. 24). This appears to be the opinion of a barrister and the court case of Franklyn and the Master and Brethren of St. Cross (1779) is quoted as evidence.[6] But Mr. Egerton set out to annoy his parishioner in a most un-Christian manner. A lithograph, engraved in Paris in 1797, shows a field behind The Mount scattered with heaps of wood, with a man hired to sharpen cross-cut saws, a wind-driven propeller operating a noisy rattle, a fox and a dog tethered just out of reach of each other so that they barked continuously and whenever the dog moved a large bell rang from a hastily-erected pitched roof set at ground level. Also shown is a huge pile of burning bones, presumably from a slaughter-house, which would have created an abominable smell (fig. 25). The field had been bought by the rector specifically to set up the nuisance, all of which was intended to drive Mr. Wickstead from his home and to cause him maximum distress. The lithograph is headed '*In perpetuam Offensae Memoriam*' (In everlasting Memory of the Offence) and below are the words

Et neque jam Cineres ejactatamque Favillam
Ferre potest; calidoque involvitur undique fume

(Nor can he bear any longer the ashes and the embers cast forth, and he is enveloped in hot smoke on all sides', an apt quotation from Ovid, the Latin poet (43BC–17AD).[7] Not surprisingly Mr Wickstead brought a successful action against the rector who was directed by the Referee, Joseph

Figure 25 Lithograph of 1797 showing the field behind The Mount bought by Francis Egerton and the nuisances which he created on it to annoy Mr. Wickstead

Lane Esq., to sell to Mr. Wickstead the field and to pay up to £700 in damages. On the copy of the lithograph, which the present authors were privileged to borrow, a hand-written paragraph had been added: 'The various nuisances set up against Mr. Wickstead Esq by the Rev. Fra. Egerton at Whitchurch for which an action was brought by the former against the latter who was directed by the referee Jo. Lane Esq to sell to Mr. W. the field on which the nuisances were set up and bought by him for the purpose. To pay 6 or 700£ damages and costs and restore the house as it was before the nuisances which had obliged Mr. W. to change the rooms' — there follows a squiggle which seems to suggest that the wording was unfinished.[8]

But Francis Henry Egerton had another, much kinder, side to his character. He concerned himself greatly with the plight of the poor and in a print-out of the Act for 'The Better Relief and Employment ... of the Poor ... of Whitchurch' in 1792 is a hand-written amendment signed by the Clerk to the Committee of the Vestry and seven members including William Wickstead, deputy chairman, refusing aid, assistance or relief to anyone who kept a dog or dogs. But Mr. Egerton would not allow the clause to go forward. It was read, however, in the Committee of the House of Commons who unanimously rejected it as 'unnecessary, cruel and arbitrary'. It had been drawn up by Mr. Wickstead and Mr. Knight and a note after the signatures criticises them for inserting the words 'after the space of three days'. The note ends 'Without these words Starving, that is to say Death through famine was to be the moderate punishment of a pauper who kept a dog in the parish of Whitchurch'. Presumably the clerk is quoting Mr. Egerton's words.[9] A little earlier Mr. Egerton had written from his home in Grosvenor Square, London a lengthy letter to the committee regarding proposals for the Bill and concluding with the words 'Gentlemen, with regard to myself I have only one object in view, the general prosperity, welfare and accommodation of the Parish of Whitchurch. To this object (though I care little to say anything of myself) I have devoted much care, attention and trouble. I request that with the same object in view you will not hastily render this care, attention and trouble abortive ...'.[10] This letter portrays a very different man from the dissolute image his wilder exploits had suggested, although it is clear that the deputy chairman, William Wickstead and the Rector had their disagreements. Could Mr. Wickstead's attitude to the poor have been part of the reason for Mr. Egerton's unusual reaction? In fairness it should be pointed out that at that time dogs were not generally regarded with much affection and most churches employed a 'dog whipper' to keep the hallowed building free from stray mutts. Certainly St. Alkmund's at Whitchurch had a reserved seat for the whipper near the reading desk and the Clerk's box. A later cleric, another Egerton, had vivid recollections of the terror both to young children and dogs that was generated by the man armed with a large whip.[11] The rich were advised to 'destroy all useless dogs' and the poor were advised to 'keep no dogs for they rob your children and neighbours'.[12]

The major part of the Rector's letter was concerned with the provision of a new workhouse or 'House of Industry' for the town and surrounding area for which the parliamentary Act referred to was required. The workhouse was eventually built in 1794.[13] Part of the original building survives and serves as the office block for the present Community Hospital at Deermoss.

Eighteenth-century Whitchurch had good reason to be grateful to Mr. Egerton despite the fact that he spent more on his pet cats and dogs than many of his parishioners could have earned in a lifetime. In 1788 he paid £63 14s. 9d. for a new dog-kennel at the Rectory (figs. 26 & 27). This was designed by 'Mr. Wallace' and included £3 3s. 2d. for sinking a well and erecting a pump, a facility which the majority of Whitchurch townspeople did not enjoy. It is difficult to reconcile the two drawings which are captioned 'Mr. Wallace's plan for the dog kennel ...' and equally difficult to see where some of the others included in the 'dog kennel papers' fit into the scheme of things. One is of a moulded cornice in cyma recta and cyma reversa form, full size, 'of wood' and headed 'Plan of Roof at Do' (fig. 28). Mr. Carr's name is a pencilled addition and on the back of the paper is a rather inferior sketch of a king-post truss the tie-beam of which was to measure 20ft. 11 ins. (fig. 4). As mentioned above in Chapter Two the latter is probably that which was used to re-roof the tithe barn. Another sheet of paper with drawings which may perhaps be attributed to Carr depicts a five-barred gate captioned 'Sketch of Entrance to the Rectory' on one side and what appears to be an idio-

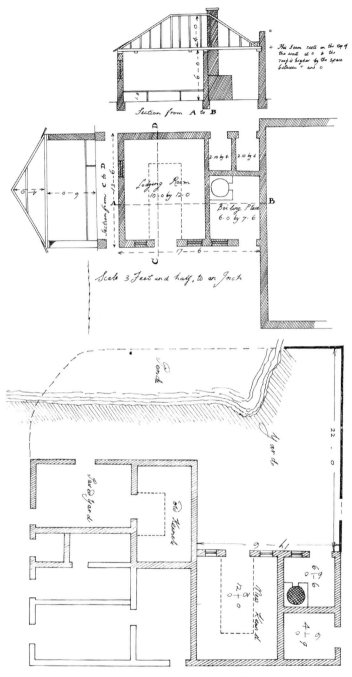

Figures 26 and 27 (above) Mr. Wallace's plan for a dog kennel at the Rectory, October 1788
Figure 28 (right) The potential cornice for the kennel (traced from the Rector's Books)

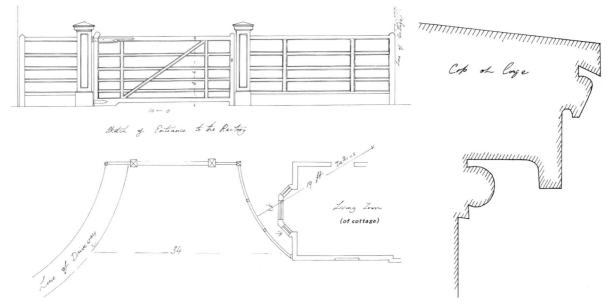

Figure 29 (above) Proposed five bar gate at the entrance to the Rectory
Figure 30 (above right, and right) Idiosyncratic cornice mouldings
(traced from the Rector's Books)

syncratic cornice moulding on the other (figs. 29 & 30). It is possible that Mr. Carr had ambitions to enhance the cornice of the house and, in addition to the large dining room which he proposed, to carry out further alterations.[14]

Egerton's eccentricities extended to having shoes made by the court shoe-maker for his pets to wear on wet days. They were dressed as men and women, drove with him in his carriage and ate at his table.[15] After the battle of Waterloo in 1815 the Rev. Egerton left England and went to live in Paris. In 1817 he bought a mansion in the Rue St. Honore which he named the 'Hotel Egerton', leaving his Whitchurch parish in the hands of curates. Indeed, as Falk states, 'At Whitchurch and Myddle the curates who had previously done three-quarters of the work for Egerton now shouldered the remainder as well.'[16] His neglect of his parish is noted in the Visitation of 1799: '... who keeps the parsonage in his own hands and has servants there, but is very little there himself'. The reports also notes that the parsonage 'is a large good house and is in good repair' and gives the living, without Marbury, as worth £1,000 per annum.[17] In 1821 the curate, Henry Morrall M.A., was given official sanction to occupy the Rectory 'during the non-residence of the said Rector'.[18] Egerton's frequent and prolonged absences must have caused difficulties in many aspects of parish affairs. In 1789 a letter presumed to be that of a barrister retained for the purpose of advising on the running of the Free Grammar School gives the opinion that if the rector is absent the feoffees (governors) should proceed without him at meetings.[19] There is much correspondence concerning his part in the school's administration, not all of it favourable. His was an impor-tant position. The statutes and ordinances of the school, revised in 1779, give the duty of the Rector and the feoffees to choose the schoolmaster who in turn chose the Usher.[20] The establishment of a Sunday School was also the responsibility of the rector, the curates and 'two of the principal inhabitants.'[21]

Further examples of his egotism and eccentricity may be given. When in Paris he had a number of medals made with his bust on one side and his name and titles on the other. The medals were enclosed in thick glass or crystal and hermetically sealed. Many were sent to England, America and parts of Europe to be deposited in the foundations of public buildings, under the piers of bridges and thrown into fountains, lakes and rivers. One of his last drives in Paris was for his servant to throw some medals into various parts of the Seine. As his chronicler comments: 'Alas, poor human nature!'[22] Many of his servants had lived with him for years but he left them nothing in his will and one who had served him for up to thirty years received only £40.[23] Yet, as recorded below, he was capable of much generosity, especially to the poor.

As mentioned above, the question of tithes and all matters pertaining to them loomed large in the rector's life, and there are many related items in the Rector's Books. Egerton was involved in a case concerning a hay tithe, at the end of which he received a bill from his solicitors for £73.[24] Another document is a bill from John Benson of the Red Lyon for six days' stabling and feed for the horses of the Commissioners (pl. 9). This came to £12 15s. 9d. Meals were also supplied to the Commissioners and wine, ale, tobacco, beer, punch and 'Negors' are itemised. 'Negors' was a hot toddy (negus) made from port or sherry, well spiced. Mr. Egerton's share is given as £6 13s. 8d, but as the bill is dated February 1748 and the name is specified as Philip Egerton, the person may not have been the subject of this chapter and it is too early for the Commissioners to be concerned with tithes.[25]

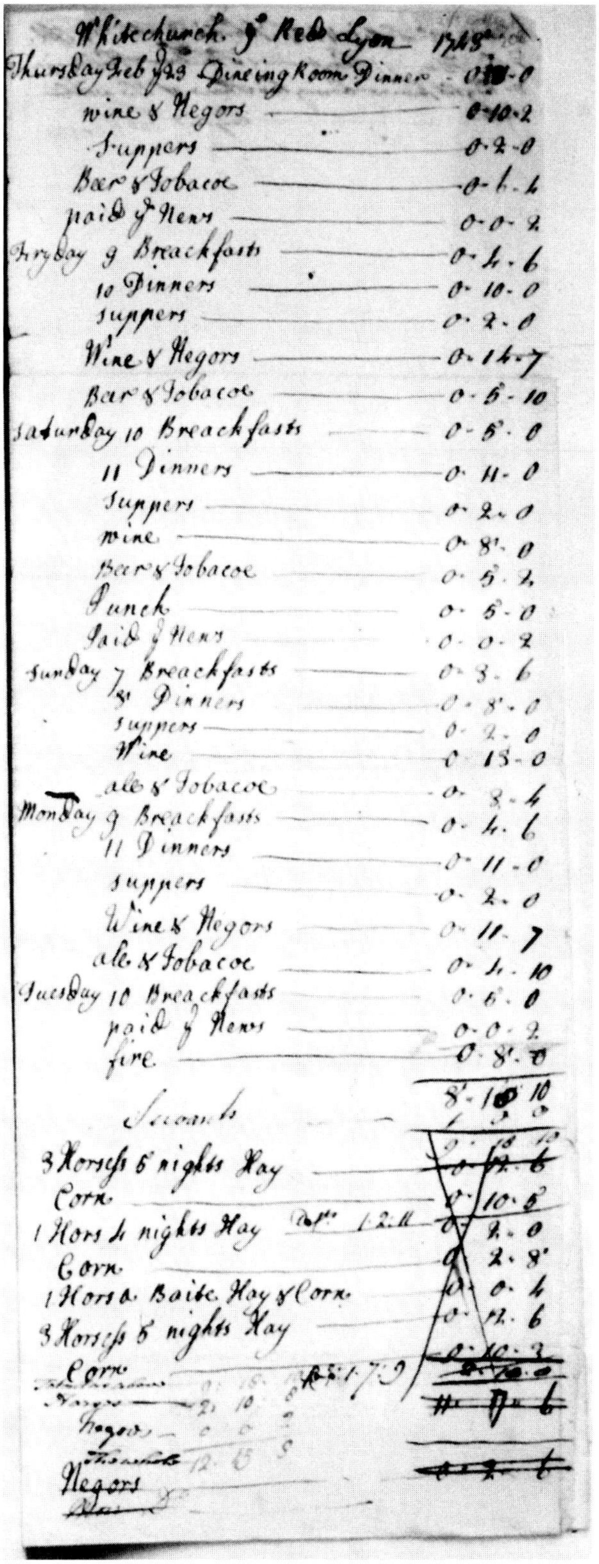

Plate 9 Bill from the Red Lyon, 1748

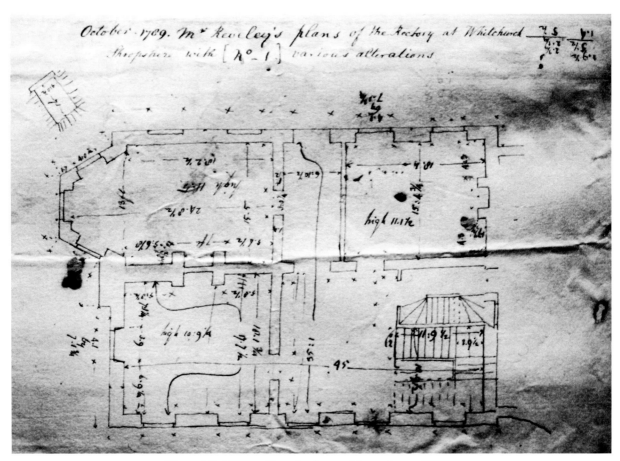

Plate 10 Willey Reveley's working plan of 1789

But in addition to the disposal of his library and the generous bequests that Francis Henry made to the British Museum he did not forget the poor of Whitchurch, leaving a legacy of £2,191 15s. 6d., the interest to be distributed yearly by the then rector. The bequest was paid in Paris to avoid questions with the Legacy Office.[26]

On the death of his brother in 1823 he succeeded to the Earldom of Bridgwater, and after years of ill-health he died in Paris on 11 February 1829 aged 72, the eighth and last Earl of Bridgwater. He was buried at Little Gaddesden, Hertfordshire, near the family seat, Ashridge.[27]

The architect, Willey Reveley (1760–1799), had been employed in 1789 to make suggestions for alterations to the Rectory, and four pages captioned 'Mr. Reveley's plans' are contained in the Rector's Book I.[28] The first of these has not been copied as it is very cluttered and is clearly a rough working plan. It is shown as a photograph (pl. 10). The written measurements tally closely with those of the present day and although the caption reads '... with various alterations' it relates more closely to an existing plan, very similar to that shown on fig. 8. The cross passage, mentioned above, is shown as existing. The second drawing is much more finished and in this it was proposed to add large bay windows to the drawing room and to what was then the dining room (present parlour) (fig. 31). The library already had such a bay. The third drawing is further complicated by the proposal to alter the dining room completely, giving it an apsed end into the hall, adding rooms on the north side, introducing free-standing ornate pillars and adding a pillared porch (fig. 32).

The configuration of the staircase is a little difficult to follow but its position is basically the same suggesting that was a respected feature and that there were no proposals to change it. This leaves unanswered the question of why, at present, the cornice on the wall to the left of the rising section stops short of the corner.

The fourth drawing is dated 1833 and will be discussed in the next chapter. In October 1789, when the first three drawings were made, Francis Henry Egerton would have been in office for eight years.

It was also proposed to provide Mr. Egerton with a water closet in June 1785 (fig. 33). This drawing shows that the staircase was screened off by a partition wall and that the cross passage was in place. The water closet was to have a mahogany seat and a proper cistern. The estimate from a 'Mr. Wallace' was £56 8s., but this included a cost of £8 16s. 5d. for digging out a well. The location of this water closet is shown on the plan, but a pencilled note on the same document and dated 1833 proposed a second water closet at ground level by converting the butler's

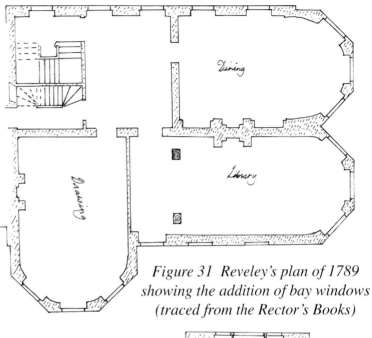

Figure 31 Reveley's plan of 1789 showing the addition of bay windows (traced from the Rector's Books)

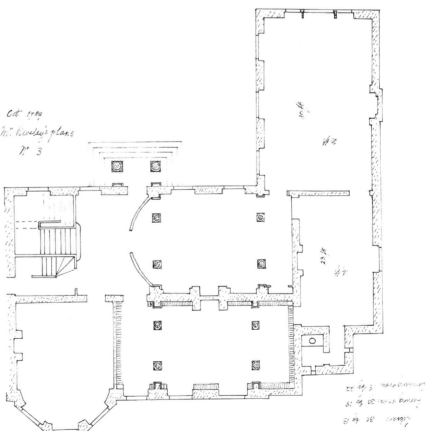

Figure 32 Reveley's plan of 1789 showing a larger remodelling of the building (traced from the Rector's Books)

pantry to that use. A partition of wood and a swing door 'would deaden all sound'.[29] It is thought that eventually it was located in the position shown on the 1841 glebe terrier plan (fig. 40).

The second closet was for a successor of Egerton, Charles Maitland Long, whose incumbency is discussed in the next chapter and whose interesting ancestry is given in Chapter 7.

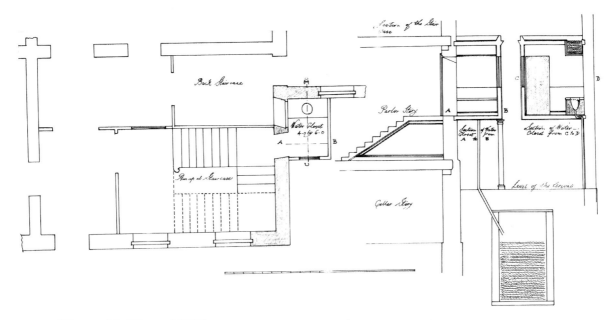

Figure 33 Plan of 1785 to construct a water closet (traced from the Rector's Books)

5   The Nineteenth Century

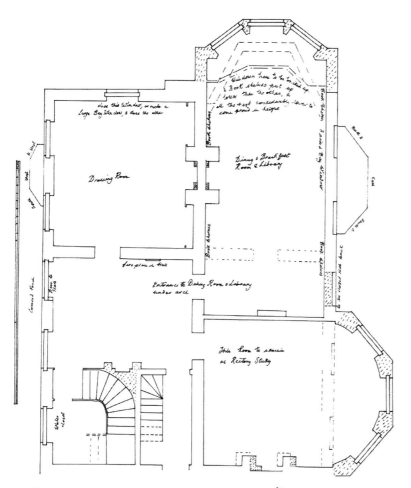

The Rev. Francis Henry Egerton was succeeded as Rector by Edward Tatham (1829–1833) followed by Charles Maitland Long who thought to improve the Rectory and employed Willey Reveley's son, Henry Willey (*c*.1789–1875), to make suggestions. His plan, captioned 'Mr. Reveley's plans No. 4' in the Rector's Book 1 (fig. 34), show an altered staircase, the apsed end gone from the dining room, alterations made to the canted bay window at the north end of the library and with the doorway in the rear wall at the end of the cross passage bricked up. Appended to Henry Willey Reveley's plans is a note:

Figure 34 (left)
'Mr. Reveley's
plans No. 4' with
further options for
remodelling the
Rectory (traced
from the Rector's
Books)

Suggested alterations would not cost much and would I think be fully sufficient. The stables might be fenced off with a high close paling in front with holly, laurel etc. The carriage road should enter from the Bargates [a revival of the original plan on the Faculty], pass the lawn and come over the moat immediately in front of the Hall door. The present road should remain for carting of coals etc. I should not take down the barn, but plant it off. In short plant off stables, House and the School [the old Grammar School in Bargates] and plant one or two clumps of trees, say six, in the park paling on the bank near the churchyard. The appearance of the House would be greatly improved by altering it into Old English style and colouring it and I would remove the parapet wall and hopper by which the house is often flooded.[1]

Other ideas for modernisation included plans for another water closet, as noted above. It is not known whether any of these 'improvements' were carried out. Certainly the 'Old English' style was never inflicted on the house, and it still retains its handsome Georgian façade. There is no evidence of a water closet under the stairs and the approach road is still from Claypit Street.

The Reveleys were not the only architects to submit plans for alterations and improvements to the rectory. Charles Porden (1790–1863) was employed by Charles Maitland Long and a folder of his plans, five in all, survives in the Rectors' Book.[2] These are very detailed, beautifully drawn and each is signed with his full name. They show sweeping proposals, much more extensive than Reveley's, and altering the front of the house drastically (figs. 35, 36, 37, 38, 39). Mrs. Long was to have a 'boudoir', there was to be an 'oratory' off the library, the staircase was to have a curving walled approach, dressing rooms were to be introduced, a hexagonal 'cabinet' (presumably an alternative name for the oratory) is shown and the children were to have a play area on the lead roof over the pantries below. Not all these features are shown on the same drawing; each has variations and a considerable amount of time and effort must have been expended on them.

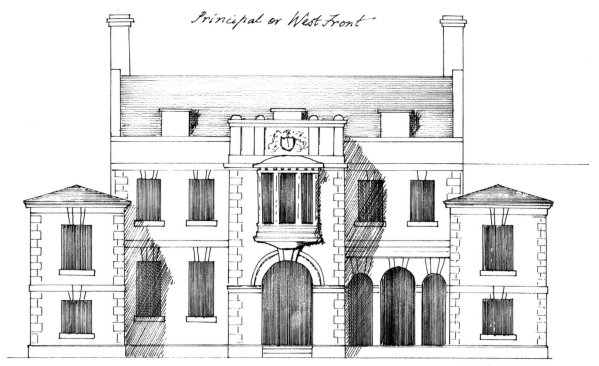

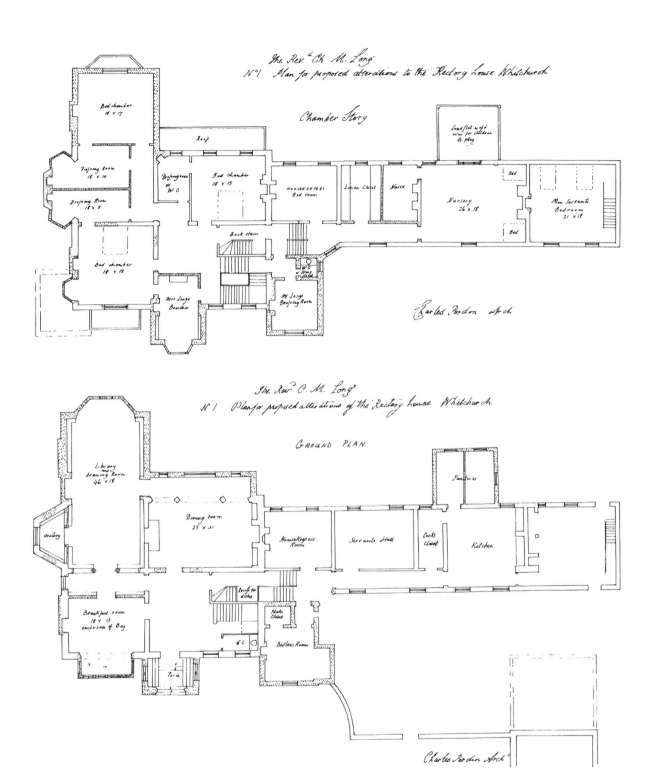

Plans produced by Charles Porden (traced from the Rector's Books)
Figure 35 (left) The Principal or West Front
Figures 36 and 37 (above) The Ground and Chamber Storeys

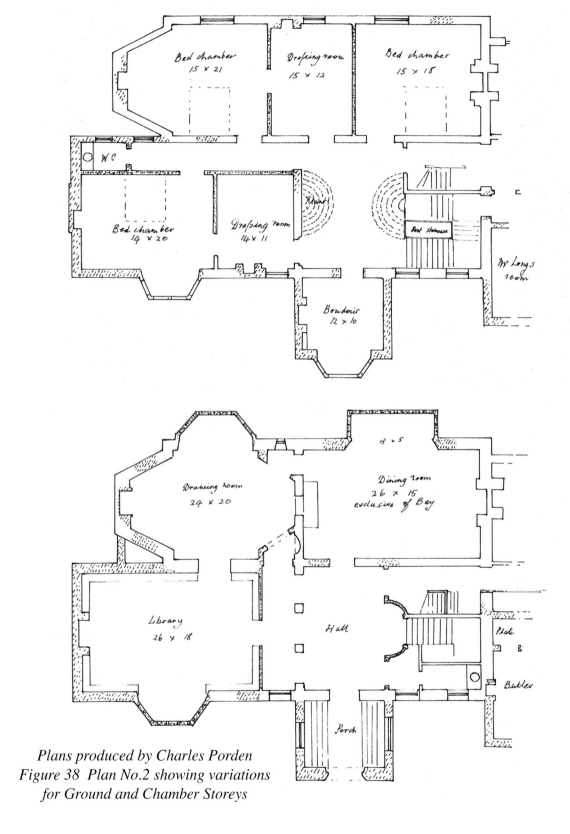

Plans produced by Charles Porden
Figure 38 Plan No.2 showing variations
for Ground and Chamber Storeys

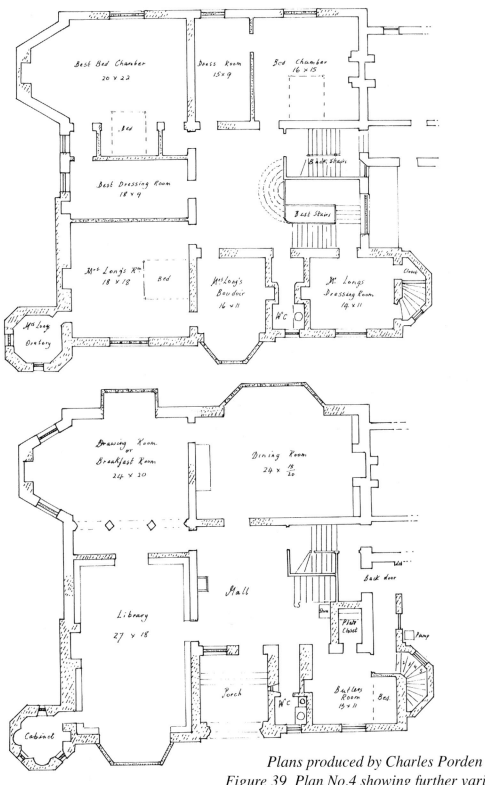

Best Bed Chamber
20 x 22

Dress Room
15 x 9

Bed Chamber
16 x 15

Bed

Porch

Back Stairs

Best Dressing Room
18 x 9

Best Stairs

Mrs Long's Rm.
18 x 18

Bed

Mrs Long's
Boudoir
16 x 11

WC

Mr. Long's
Dressing Room
14 x 11

Closet

Mrs Long
Oratory

Drawing Room
or
Breakfast Room
24 x 20

Dining Room
24 x $\frac{15}{20}$

Back door

Hall

S

Stove

Plate
Closet

Pump

Library
27 x 18

Porch

WC

Butlers
Room
15 x 11

Bed.

Cabinet

Plans produced by Charles Porden
Figure 39 Plan No.4 showing further variations
for Ground and Chamber Storeys

37

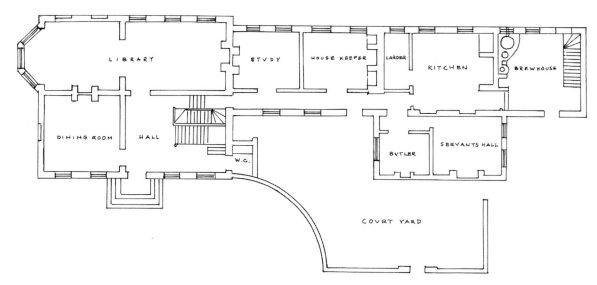

Figure 40 'Plan of Whitchurch Rectory House with the alterations and additions as in the year A.D. 1841', as included in the 1841 Glebe Terrier (traced from the Rector's Books)

The plans are not dated but it seems likely that they were drawn up *c*.1841. A Terrier dated 9 September of that year states that 'A plan of the rectory as altered in 1841 is included' (fig. 40). This is so like the Faculty plan (fig. 8) and, indeed, the present plan (fig. 12) that it emphasises how little the rectory has changed over the years.[3] A fifth plan (fig. 41), not included in the folder but possibly also from Porden, has only initials for the signature and these are difficult to interpret. They could be 'GTW' – perhaps one of Porden's staff – and represent the missing number three in the sequence. In the typed index under 'Loose Papers' in the Rector's Books is a document entitled 'Rough plan of library, reading closet, tapestry room, bedchambers and nursery on the chamber floor' Sadly this document is missing, but the fact that a 'tapestry room' and a 'reading closet' are included perhaps reflects the lifestyle of the Long family. The Reveleys and Charles

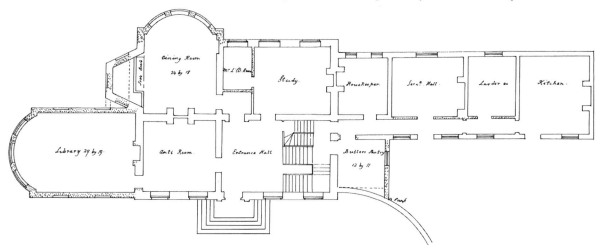

Figure 41 The missing plan No.3 from the folder, probably produced by one of Porden's staff (traced from the Rector's Books)

Porden were architects with a nationwide reputation, as was John Carr if, as suspected, he was of the well-known Yorkshire family. The latter point is expanded below.

It seems clear from the above that Charles Maitland Long had more than a passing interest in architecture. He was also closely involved with the provision of the chapel of St. Catherine in Dodington in 1836, which was endowed by Catherine, Countess of Bridgwater. Happily, though now redundant, the building survives. The Shrewsbury architect Edward Haycock, who had an extensive practice in Shropshire and was also County Surveyor, was chosen. Haycock favoured the Grecian style and the Rector's Book contains a delightful coloured painting of the front elevation with Haycock's name attached. There is also a letter from Haycock to Charles Maitland Long concerning an additional entrance to be made in the side of the chapel.[4] Mr. Long was succeeded by the Rev. William Henry Egerton M.A. on 20 February 1846. He held office for sixty-three years, retiring in February 1909. He had been born in Malpas on 13 November 1811 and died on 16 March 1910 in his hundredth year. Like his predecessors, Rector Egerton lived the life of a country gentleman. The servants' quarters adjoining the main house were comprehensive and included a kitchen, servants' hall, pantry, larder and scullery with a large game and meat larder and coal-house outside. There was an underground Ice-house in the grounds where meat and other comestibles could be preserved in blocks of ice and there was stabling for three horses with hay-lofts, a saddle-room and a coach-house. The Ice-house survives (see plan, fig. 42) and catalogued in the same folder in the Rector's Book I is a composite drawing of alternative designs for iron gates which, presumably, gave access to the whole complex (fig. 43). The stable block was restored in the 1980s for residential use. In addition to his duties to the church Rector Egerton did much to awaken interest in the long history of his adopted town, writing many articles for the *Transactions* of the Shropshire Archaeological Society, particularly on the life, death and burial of John Talbot, 1st Earl of Shrewsbury, a national hero of the Hundred Years' War, foe of St. Joan of Arc and a major character in Shakespeare's

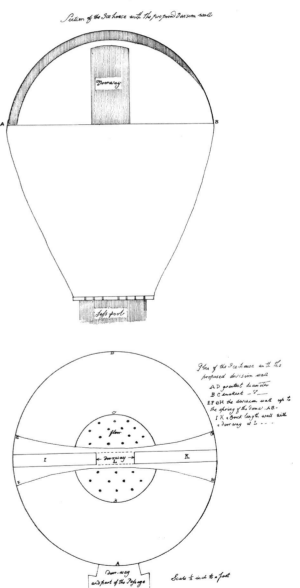

Figure 42 Plan of the surviving Ice-house (traced from the Rector's Books)

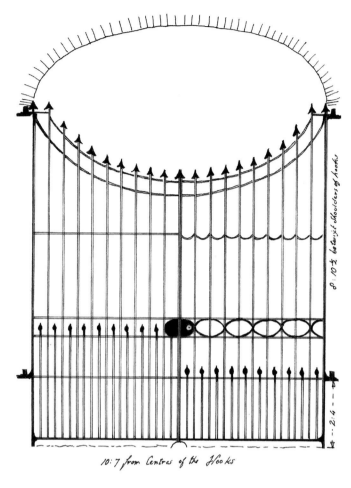

*Figure 43 Drawings produced for gates
(traced from the Rector's Books)*

Henry V1 Part I. Talbot's bones found a final resting place in the church where there is a fine monument to him, (see fig. 3) and his heart lies beneath a stone in the porch entrance.[5]

Born in 1811, William Henry Egerton lived through the reigns of George III, George IV, William IV, Queen Victoria, and Edward VII. In a lecture given to the 'Whitchurch Conversazione' in 1896 he recalled his memories of the peace celebrations in 1815 after the defeat of Napoleon at Waterloo. He also recorded the visit to Oxford University of the Duke of Wellington who received that body's 'highest honour'. There was, he says, 'great enthusiasm amongst the students'.[6] Lectures were promoted in Whitchurch. A Terrier dated 23 July 1849 includes details of an annual payment made to the rector for 'maintaining a weekly lecture on Thursdays'. The amount varied, but it was specified in the will of James Phillips Esq, dated 24 April 1661 and the sum of £54 12s was paid into the fund in 1848.[7]

ARCHITECTURAL ASSESSMENT

In Chapter Three the Old Rectory is described as 'simplified Georgian classic' and this fits the form in which it was built and largely remains to this day. Perhaps this section should be sub-titled 'What might have been'. Certainly the numerous drawings with suggestions for alterations make an interesting study and emphasise the richness of the living at Whitchurch. The incumbents would have had to choose and pay the architects and pay for what alterations they wanted done. The important point about the architects is that they were all well-known and eminent men in their field. If, as suspected, the 'Mr Carr' was John Carr (1723–1807) of Yorkshire, then several features slot into place such as the canted bay windows, the cyma-moulded cornice, the apsed ends, his 40ft. x 20ft. room and the 18ft. square room on fig. 22, and other Palladian touches such as the iron gates (fig. 43). Carr was a 'disciple' of Lord Burlington, the leader of the Palladian movement in England, and while it is thought that his work was confined to the north, perhaps he was tempted to look at Shropshire. Palladianism is not common in Shropshire, although a few examples may be quoted, and a Carr/Palladian house would, at least, have partially filled a gap.[8]

Willey Reveley (1760–1799), another Yorkshireman, favoured the Greek style of classicism, particularly the Orders.[9] This would account for the preponderance of free-standing pillars shown on figs. 31 and 32. At this point it may be useful to mention that at High Hatton Hall which, as mentioned above, has a very similar staircase, there are two non-structural pillars in the drawing room. In attributing 'Mr Reveley's plan no 4' (fig. 34) to his son Henry Willey it is the date of 1833 that is taken as evidence. Some doubt arises here as Henry Willey worked professionally in Cape Town and later in Australia, not returning to England until he was past retirement.[10] Perhaps there is some mistake in the date on the drawing although it all seems to be in the same hand, but it is noticeable that on the 4th plan all the ornamental pillars have gone.

Charles Porden (1790–1863) worked for ten years for Sir William Tite, the architect of the Royal Exchange in London.[11] Tite had an eclectic range and Porden's suggestions for the Old Rectory perhaps reflect this influence, especially his design for the frontage in the 'old English' style, in other words 'Gothick'.

There remains the question of the identity of the original architect. As mentioned above, Samuel Turner is a strong candidate but Thomas Farnolls Pritchard has an equal claim. Pritchard's life and work is well documented and a working drawing book survives.[12] While there is nothing in the written records to associate him directly with the Old Rectory or with Whitchurch, a link with the town, particularly with a house in Green End, has been discovered, and there are, of course, gaps in our knowledge of his achievements and particularly of his early work.[13] The chief feature which links Pritchard to the Old Rectory is the staircase, described above, and its similarity to the one at High Hatton Hall, known to have come from the Pritchard practice. It is worth emphasising that the pattern of the balusters, three to a step, two twisted and one plain, is typical of Pritchard's carefully crafted work and that a valuation for the Guildhall in Ludlow, another known commission of his, records both square and turned balusters being made.[14] But there are other features such as the canted bays, and at High Hatton he used them with exuberance, as he did at Downton Hall, Croft Castle, Shipton Hall and Hatton Grange, although in the latter they may be later additions.[15] Two other features favoured by Pritchard are the eared surround to doorways and fireplaces and the egg-and-dart or egg-and-leaf motifs. In the parlour/morning-room of the Old Rectory are the remains of an original fireplace. It has been badly mutilated and at some time a later fireplace has been built in front of it, but it is clear that it had a classically moulded mantel-shelf and an eared surround edged with egg-and-dart moulding (fig. 44). Another fireplace of similar, though not identical, design is shown

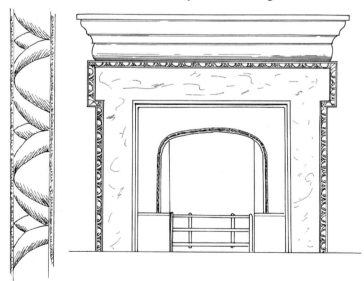

Figure 44 Reconstruction of Parlour fireplace and detail of its egg-and-dart moulding

on the photograph of William Henry Egerton in old age (pl. 11). This must have been taken in the drawing room, and it also shows part of the huge collection of books about which there was so much concern later. Pritchard used both hallmarks extensively and for Mr. Samuel Egerton at Tatton Park he designed a fireplace with egg-and-dart moulding edging an eared surround, and there are several others in his drawing book.[16] It is worth noting that in 17 Green End there are two Pritchardian fireplaces, each with egg-and-leaf ornament.[17]

There seems to have been a proliferation of coach-houses at the Old Rectory. One is mentioned in the 1612 terrier, noted above, and Samuel Turner's plan taken in 1749 has a coach-house labelled as such within the moated area (fig. 5). It is possible that at one time part of the gate-house was also used for this purpose, and the building opposite the tithe barn has one high arched double doorway and a lower one, perhaps for a smaller vehicle, in the long brick wall which, as mentioned above, was probably part of the 1749 building programme.

Plate 11 William Henry Egerton in old age, c.1907, from a photograph in the vestry. Note the eighteenth-century fireplace and part of the vast library

6   THE TWENTIETH CENTURY

On his retirement in 1909 Mr. Egerton was succeeded by Sydney Dugdale whose brother, Major Dugdale, lived nearby in Terrick Hall. One of the rector's first requests was that he might get rid of the library at the rectory which at that time had increased to over 3,000 volumes. He was advised by the diocesan registry that there were legal difficulties and so nothing was done. The library had been left by Jane, Countess Dowager of Bridgwater, who in 1707, having purchased the books from the executors of the Rev. Clement Sankey for £305, left it 'for ever' to the rectors of Whitchurch. The collection was later augmented by Francis Henry Egerton who left £4 9s. 6d. per annum for its maintenance and a sum of £150, the interest on which was to be used to buy more books. This, from all accounts, was never implemented. It was Mr. Dugdale's successor, the Rev. Hugh Hanmer who, in 1923, removed the volumes from the house and stored them in a loft above the stables.[1]

Hugh Hanmer accepted the living in 1920. By this time the rectory was thought to be too big, inconvenient and expensive to maintain. In a Terrier, not dated and dealing with many different matters, is the transcript of a letter from two sisters, Mary Ann and Dora Jane Kent who lived at Green End House, (now Weston House Nursing Home), dated 1 July 1922 and offering to purchase 'Highfields', a more modern house in Tarporley Road, for use as a Rectory (pl. 12). 'Highfields' was built in 1877 for Robert Thursfield Smith, a partner with his brother William Henry in the engineering and iron foundry business which produced, among other things, the well-known Dutch barns which bear the characteristic blue metal labels, and who were, with Joyce's clockworks, Whitchurch's main employers.[2] The Kent sisters would make a gift of it to the parish subject to themselves receiving 5% interest on their capital outlay during their joint lives and that of the survivor, and subject also to the Old Rectory being sold and money from

Plate 12 Highfields, the gift of the Misses Kent.
This was used as the Rectory 1923–1972

that sale used to pay for the transfer of Highfields from the Kents to the benefice.[3] The ladies were then aged seventy-six and seventy-eight and as the matter had been causing concern to the rector, the church-wardens, the parochial church council and the parishioners for some time, this generous offer was gratefully accepted. The Misses Kent duly bought Highfields for £3,620, and their gift is commemorated on a plaque in St. Alkmund's (pl.13).

THIS TABLET IS ERECTED
TO COMMEMORATE THE GIFT IN THE YEAR 1923
OF THE NEW RECTORY IN TARPORLEY ROAD BY THE
MISSES MARY ANNE KENT AND DORA JANE KENT
OF GREEN END HOVSE WHITCHVRCH AND IN
GRATEFVL APPRECIATION OF MANY GIFTS BY
THEM TO THE CHVRCH AND PARISH.

Plate 13 Tablet in St. Alkmund's church commemorating the gift of Highfields

The administrators of Queen Anne's Bounty — an ecclesiastical fund founded in 1704 to augment small livings to build parsonage houses and generally make grants for church purposes — were also involved and they stipulated that some of the money from the sale of the Old Rectory was to be used to put Highfields into proper repair.[4]

At the auction on 2 March 1923 the Old Rectory failed to sell. Afterwards the Rector, Hugh Hanmer, discussed the matter with his brother, Richard, who lived at Sheepy Lodge near Atherstone, and Richard offered to purchase the Old Rectory and the Glebe at valuation and to transfer the same to his brother for a lesser amount. This was done, the figures being £1,950 for the house and £1,800 for the land. The conveyance is dated 23 July 1923. But Hugh Hanmer continued to live in the Old Rectory, in reality becoming his own landlord and leasing Highfields to James Graham Chaplin DSO for four years at a rent of £115 per annum 'until such time as it is required for a Rectory'.[5]

Extracts from the sale particulars prepared by Frank Lloyd & Sons at the Victoria Hotel, Whitchurch give a picture of the house and grounds at this time:

> LOT 1 The Residence possesses an imposing entrance and contains a large long hall communicating with dining room, drawing room and morning room whilst connecting with the side entrance are study and schoolroom. There are eight principal bed and dressing rooms approached by a staircase of good width. 2 bathrooms, lavatory and housemaids' pantry, store room and store cupboard. Approached by a secondary staircase are 2 bedrooms and a further 5 bedrooms on the 2nd floor. The Domestic department consists of kitchen, servants' hall, pantry, larder and scullery. Outside premises include a large game and meat larder, coal houses etc.
>
> Town's water supplied and Company's gas laid on. The drainage has recently been improved and modernised.
>
> Garage for 2 cars, storeroom and lofts. Stabling for 3 horses, saddle room and lofts.
>
> The Pleasure Grounds and Gardens are of a natural and artistic character and the undulations caused by the existence of the old moat crossed by a rustic garden bridge. Lawns and tennis courts are adjoining surrounded by a park-like paddock of 7 acres.
>
> A most productive kitchen garden with greenhouse, potting shed and frames. The land is rich in old pasture and is let on a yearly tenancy to Messrs Willis Bros.
>
> Farm buildings are in two ranges on either side of the farmyard.

On its western boundary this Lot presents an important frontage line of about 150 feet to Bargates.

Tithe Rent Charge (sum apportioned).

£1 Land Tax About £1 3s. 5d.

The geographical situation of the property is most favourable being within half a mile of Whitchurch station, an important London & North Western Railway junction and Great Western Railway terminus, which bring Chester, Shrewsbury and Crewe within easy reach and takes in the whole of North and Central Wales.

It is a good centre for Hunting with Sir Watkin Williams Wynn's, the Cheshire, the North Shropshire, and the North Staffordshire Packs.

Special Conditions of Sale

The books which are now housed in the room over the stable of the said residence are held by the Rector for the time being of the parish of Whitchurch for the benefit of the parish. The purchaser of Lot 1 shall allow the books to remain in the said room free of rent or charge for storage until September 30th 1923 or to such earlier date on which the same can be disposed of and the purchaser will use his best endeavours to protect the same books.

Not to use the Dwelling House or any part of land or an existing future building thereon for the purpose of a Roman Catholic church, or as an R.C. school, convent, monastery or institution or as a Lunatic Asylum or home for Incurables or as a Slaughter House or for the purpose of any offensive noisy or dangerous trade, business pursuit or occupation. No building shall be erected within 60 feet from the boundary churchyard wall.[6]

It is emphasised that the above are extracts only. There were two other Lots concerning pasture land and a field, both of which belonged to the rectory, and the whole area encompassed 34 acres. The consent of the Patron, the Right Honourable Lord Brownlow was needed in addition to the approval of the Ecclesiastical Commissioners for England. The books of the rector's library were eventually moved to the new rectory in Tarporley Road where they were stored in an outside building until c.1975 when they were placed in the care of the Shropshire County Library. In c.1990 the Library was moved to the new Shropshire Records and Research Centre (now Shropshire Archives) where they are kept in controlled conditions.

Mr. Hanmer and his family lived at Selattyn and let the Old Rectory to tenants or sub-tenants, one of whom was General Sir Thomas Astley Cubitt, Commander in the Western Territorial Division and later Governor of Bermuda. He and his wife had six children, though not all from one marriage, the eldest of whom was Veronica who later married Captain W.H. ('Tich') Bamfield. When an elderly lady living in a Shrewsbury nursing home she gave an interview to one of the authors of this book, and spoke most eloquently of her life at the Old Rectory. She loved the old house and said that the moment she entered it she felt that she had 'come home'. The gist of the interview is as follows:

I was born in 1908. My father was Bernard Grissell [Lt.-Col. Bernard Grissell DSO who was killed in the First World War] but he died when I was nine. Astley Cubitt was my step-father and his office was in Shrewsbury in the building now known as the Lord Hill Hotel. We lived in Whitchurch in the Old Rectory. Previously we had lived in Brighton where I went to school. I was about nineteen when we moved to Whitchurch, and this would be about 1927.

The drawing room was on the left and had two windows. The entrance hall was on the right. My parents' bedroom was upstairs, second on the left. The maids' bedrooms were in the attics. There was a laundry room.

We kept a cook, housemaid, manservant, nanny, groom, one gardener and a daily help. I remember a nanny dying, aged 26, in a 'flu epidemic. There was a good kitchen garden, but no farm — we were not farmers but we had horses and I had my own riding horse and a bicycle. I was allowed to have a fire in my bedroom, but I had to attend to it myself.

My mother was not good with servants, but dinner parties were frequent and we had a full social life. My father had a chauffeur-driven car and he went daily to his office in Shrewsbury.

There were dances in Whitchurch in the Town Hall and I always went to the Hunt Ball. We were members of three hunts, Sir Watkin Wynn's, the Tanatside, and the Cheshire, and my father kept two hunters. I also liked the cinema.

We all attended church. The rector was Mr Griffiths [William Charles Griffiths M.A.] and he lived in the new Rectory in Tarporley Road.

We were all involved with charities and 'good works' generally. One of my tasks was to read aloud to the old people in Deermoss [the old workhouse]. Major Lambert of Ash Grove suggested this.

I remember the gypsies who camped at Prees Heath, particularly how, when one of their community died, their possessions would be heaped into their caravan and the whole lot burned. I also remember the Italians coming to Whitchurch, particularly the Fulgoni family.[7] They were all involved with the food trade.

The house was the loveliest that I ever knew, but I deplored the additions. It was said to be haunted, but I only recall one experience when I was alone in the house except for the maids. The dogs were suddenly petrified and crouched by my door, howling. But it never happened again.

We left Whitchurch when my father was promoted to Commander in Aldershot. I was then about twenty-two and I married shortly afterwards.

As her obituary reveals, Veronica was a remarkable lady who had a happy and adventurous life. A great friend of the late Dame Freya Stark, the traveller and writer, with whom she explored places in Iraq forbidden to women, she had great breadth of knowledge and generosity of spirit. In retirement in Shrewsbury she used her talents to benefit her chosen county in many ways.[8]

Although the family only occupied the Old Rectory for about three or four years, as may be seen from Veronica's recollections, her years there left such an impression on her that at the age of ninety-two she was able to provide a vignette of life in a pre-Second World War provincial town for a middle-class family of means.

The house continued to be let to military personnel until 1933 when Mr. Hanmer put it up for sale by auction at the Victoria Hotel by Frank Lloyd & Sons on 28 April. The sale particulars are very similar to those of ten years previously, although the house was now centrally heated and the tithe barn was in use as loose boxes. Again, the choice of three packs of hounds is emphasised although 'easy access to many important golf courses' is also stressed. The last tenant was a Captain Macdonell who later joined the 9th Lancers at Bedford Barracks, Colinton, Midlothian.[9] The house and grounds were sold with vacant possession to the Rev. E.A. Dentith. At the time

Mr. Dentith was the curate of St. Luke's church in Oswestry and later he became the vicar of Fauls Green, near Prees. His parents, Mr. R.A. Dentith with his wife Louisa, and their unmarried daughters came to live in the Old Rectory. Mr. Dentith senior died two years later[10] but his family stayed on in the house where two of his four daughters ran a small kindergarten school.

A former pupil, Mrs. Olive Walker (*née* Wainwright) has supplied the authors with first-hand knowledge of the school. The following is her account verbatim:

> There were about one dozen children of varying ages at the Old Rectory Kindergarten. We were all taught in one classroom by Miss Gladys Dentith. The classroom was in the servants' quarters on the right of the house. In summer we were taught outside on the lawns, the desks were sometimes outside. On other occasions we had a spelling bee sitting in a swinging hammock. We went home at lunch times, but if necessary we could take sandwiches. We took these to the tennis court seats in summer to eat. The tennis courts were over a small wooden bridge over the moat, now empty, past the vegetable garden, and they looked onto the London Road.
>
> At play times we rode bicycles or scooters around the paved area outside the coach house, on the left of the archway as you approach the house from the long drive.
>
> One of the main rooms in the house had a partition and this was opened at Christmas for our Christmas party. One year a hamper of dressing-up clothes was provided and a very large cracker with a small gift for everyone.
>
> There was also a train set laid out in a small room for the boys to play with and also there was a rocking horse in the classroom.
>
> We would be taken into the garden to collect moss to make miniature gardens and to look at birds' nests.
>
> When Edward Dentith sold the Rectory about 1939 we moved to Green End, opposite to Mr. Ayton's, the dentist. Miss Dentith was already engaged to Mr. Holmes and she soon gave up to get married.

Plate 14 Pupils at the Rectory Kindergarten c.1937. Teacher: Miss G.M. Dentith. (Photo courtesy of Mrs. Olive Walker [née Wainwright] seated on right)

Olive's last report before the school had to move survives and is reproduced as fig. 45. The number of subjects taught might appear daunting to modern educationists, but it also reflects great credit on one little girl. At the outbreak of war the house was requisitioned (not sold, as Olive states).

In 1974 one of the Miss Dentiths, now Mrs. Pridding, gave a talk to the children of Class 4 in Whitchurch Junior School, describing life at the old Rectory as she knew it. Later the children were taken to visit it and the essays that they wrote afterwards are preserved in the archives of the Whitchurch History and Archaeology Group. Their teacher at the time was the late Mrs. Joan Young and the children were mostly eight years of age. It is clear that the children were most impressed with the project and their efforts are indeed, praiseworthy. Mrs. Pridding had described how the garden at the Old Rectory was beautifully kept with neat lawns, well-planted flower beds, clipped hedges and two immaculate tennis courts. There was a rose garden, an orchard and a kitchen garden which supplied fresh vegetables for the family. There was always a plentiful supply of evergreens to decorate the church at Easter and Christmas. She recalled that her mother, Mrs. Louisa Dentith, had planted the formal flower beds with red, white and blue flowers to celebrate the coronation of King George VI in May 1937. By this time the house was centrally

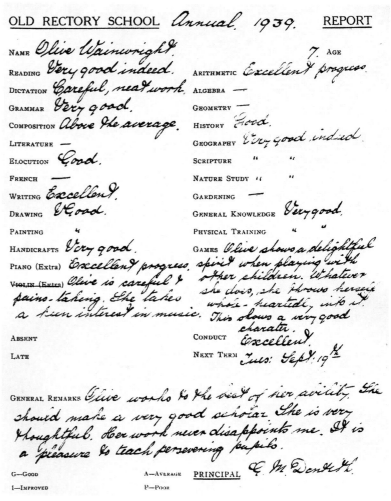

Figure 45 Olive Walker's [née Wainwright] last report before the school closed

heated by a coke boiler in the cellar, but the family did not own a refrigerator. Meat, fish and other perishable foods were kept cool on a slate slab in an outside store.

The Dentith family owned the house throughout the war, although it had been requisitioned by the government. In 1955 the property was sold to the late Mr. Roger Hooper. Whilst still active he carried on various enterprises at the Old Rectory, including its use as headquarters for the Heavy Horse Preservation Society and latterly as storage for his stock of second-hand books which he retailed from a small shop in the High Street. Sadly he neglected the house which became semi-derelict and he made some injudicious sales of land and premises, including the gate-house, which have resulted in fragmentation and difficulties of access.

In 1973/4 the present Rectory was built in the churchyard and the Rev. David Jenkins with his wife and family, moving from the old 'Highfields', were the first to occupy it.

7　RECTORS OF WHITCHURCH

The new church — probably built after the Conquest and perhaps after 1086 — which caused the Domesday vill of 'Westune' to be renamed Whitchurch[1] doubtless owed its existence to an early Norman lord of the manor. Thus the advowson or patronage of the church — the right to present a suitable man, qualified by holy orders, to the bishop for institution to the rectory — passed down to the founder's successors as lords of the manor.

Whitchurch manor has always been in aristocratic hands.[2] The Conqueror conferred it on his kinsman William de Warenne, created earl of Surrey shortly before his death in 1088. Probably at some time before 1148, when Warenne's inheritance passed to an heiress, Whitchurch had been subinfeudated to a cadet branch of the Warennes who, though they held other lands under the earl in Norfolk, adopted the surname Whitchurch (*Blancminster*). The cadet line held it until, in turn, their male line failed *c.*1260 and their lands were divided among coheiresses. Whitchurch was eventually reunited, in 1306, in the hands of Fulk le Strange, grandson of the last Warenne (or Whitchurch) of Whitchurch, whose mother had married Bevis de Knovill (d.1307) *en secondes noces* some time after 1277. The manor then remained with the Stranges of Blakemere, summoned to Parliament as Lords Strange of Blakemere from 1309, until the death in 1413 of their heiress Ankaret (*née* le Strange), Dowager Lady Furnivalle and relict of Richard, Lord Talbot. Thereafter it passed down to her Talbot descendants (Earls of Shrewsbury from 1442) until 1598. That year the manor was bought by Sir Thomas Egerton, lord keeper of the great seal and later, on his creation as Baron Ellesmere, lord chancellor 1603–17. The manor continued in the Egerton family until the death of the Dowager Countess of Bridgwater, widow of the 7th earl, in 1849. After some litigation the Egertons' inheritance passed in 1853 to their kinsmen, the Earls Brownlow (from 1921 Barons Brownlow). The 6th Baron Brownlow's executors conveyed the advowson to the Bishop of Lichfield *c.*1990.[3]

For the lord of the manor the advowson of Whitchurch was a valuable piece of patronage, for the rectory was one of the richest parochial livings in Shropshire. The rectory was valued at £13 6s. 8d. in 1291. It was worth at least £19 8s. 3d. gross in 1401–2, of which tithes provided £12 1s. 4d., offerings (from St. Alkmund's and the chapels at Blakemere and Marbury) £4 17s. 7d., and mortuaries (customary gifts from the estates of deceased parishioners) £2 9s. 4d.; the value of the glebe is not stated.[4] It was then a very comfortable living.[5] By 1535, when it was worth £50 a year,[6] it was recorded as the richest parochial benefice in the county[7] and long remained one of the best.[8] About 1830 the living's average gross income was £2,004 a year.[9] That made it the sixth most valuable parochial benefice in the diocese of Lichfield and Coventry and the fourth most valuable in Shropshire.[10] The wealth of the living was not due to extensive glebe land[11] — which in 1887 amounted to some 31½ acres, whose gross annual rental was only £94 10s.[12] — but to the fact that the rectorial tithes of what was a large parish had never been appropriated in the Middle Ages to a religious house. In the late 1930s Whitchurch was still a plum living: its gross annual income in 1939 was £1,206, most (£902) coming from tithe redemption; the glebe, then recorded as only 5 acres, was worth only £10 a year. The net income probably yields a better idea of what the rector of Whitchurch then actually received: £610 a year and his Rectory house. That was probably about half as much again than the income of most parochial incumbents. Before J.H. Hall became rector of Whitchurch in 1938 he had been vicar of Shifnal, where his net annual income had been £401 plus his Vicarage house. Moreover even that Shifnal stipend had probably been better than average, for about that time it seems that, while the Church of England authorities considered £400 p.a. suitable for a parochial incumbent, that was a target yet to be universally attained.[13] Even as late as the early 1970s Whitchurch rectory remained better than the average living, but the equalization of benefice incomes, forwarded by inflation, was achieved over the next few years[14] so that by the end of the following decade the rectory of Whitchurch was no longer distinguished by either aristocratic patronage or an ampler income than other livings.

LIST OF RECTORS

James Fraunceys, occurs 1297.[15]

Master John de Knovill, occurs 1310–11, died 1337.[16] The designation 'master' suggests that he was a graduate, and in 1310–11 he was licensed to be absent for study. He was evidently related to the Stranges (lords of the manor and patrons of the living), into which family the royal official Bevis de Knovill (d.1307) had married while sheriff of Shropshire (1274–8).

Bartholomew de Berdefeld, instituted 1337 (patron Sir John le Strange, Lord Strange of Blakemere), died 1358.[17] Given leave to study medicine at Oxford in 1354, he was then called 'Dominus' Bartholomew, which suggests that he was not yet a graduate.

Robert le Strange, instituted 1358 (patron Ankaret, Dowager Lady Strange of Blakemere).[18] Later that year Robert exchanged livings with his successor.

Nicholas of Dovaston, acquired the rectory from his predecessor in exchange for the rectory of Great Brickhill (Bucks.) in 1358.[19] Nicholas was probably a local man, known to his predecessor: from 1198 Dovaston was held in fee of the Stranges of Knockin.

John of Ludlow, instituted 1368 (patron King Edward III), exchanged livings with his successor 1388.[20]

Thomas Stanley, exchanged livings with his successor 1393.[21]

Thomas Welford, instituted 1393 (patron Richard Talbot, Lord Talbot), died 1409.[22] Welford, whose name is variously spelt (Wellefford, Wylleford), was licensed to be non-resident, and during his absence he let his living to the patron.

Roger de Thrisk, instituted 1409 (patron Ankaret, Baroness Strange of Blakemere, Dowager Lady Furnivalle).[23]

Richard Stanley, occurs 1421–3.[24]

Nicholas Wymbysh, instituted 1423 (patron John Talbot, Lord Furnivalle, Lord Strange of Blakemere, and Lord Talbot), resigned 1426.[25] The rector is almost certainly the graduate Chancery clerk (*c*.1391 and still in 1451) of that name. His resignation was effected, by notarial instrument, in Westminster Hall.

John Heyworth, B.Cn.L., instituted 1426 (patron John Talbot, Lord Furnivalle, Lord Strange of Blakemere, and Lord Talbot).[26] In 1421 this canon lawyer (d.1453) was vicar-general of the diocese of his kinsman Wm. Heyworth, Bishop of Coventry and Lichfield.

Master John Cumber, died 1441 or 1442.[27] Perhaps the John Combe, M.A., of whom little is known.

Roger Stedeman, instituted 1442 (patron John Talbot, Lord Furnivalle, Lord Strange of Blakemere, and Lord Talbot [created Earl of Shrewsbury 1442]), died 1455.[28] The patron 1423–42 was the 'English Achilles' who fought (unsuccessfully) against St. Joan of Arc at Orléans in 1429. Shakespeare described him as 'the terror of the French' (*1 Henry VI*, I. iv. 42) and gave him a major role of distinguished bravery, where the battle cry 'A Talbot! A Talbot!' (*1 Henry VI*, I. i. 128) conjures up images of a war lord becoming an English national hero. So fierce was his reputation that, according to Shakespeare, French parents would threaten naughty children with Talbot, the bogey man personified (*1 Henry VI*, I. iv. 43). Aged 70 he was killed at Castillon la Bataille, near Bordeaux, on 17 July 1453, when France defeated England in what proved to be the last battle of the Hundred Years' War. His heart is buried under the church porch, and his bones lie beneath the fine monument (restored by Countess Brownlow in 1874).

Thomas Sutton, instituted 1455 (patron John Talbot, 2nd Earl of Shrewsbury), resigned 1484 or 1485.[29] Among the graduates of this name the man likeliest to have been rector of Whitchurch is the Thomas Sutton, M.A., whom the bishop of Coventry and Lichfield collated to canonries in St. Chad's, Shrewsbury, and St. John's, Chester, in 1458. The two men may have been merely namesakes, for, as a graduate, the canon of Shrewsbury and Chester is consistently called 'Master' while the rector of Whitchurch is equally consistently called 'Dominus', the style for a non-graduate cleric. Nevertheless it seems likely that one man is indicated, and it is to be noted that his successor is variously referred to as 'Master' and 'Dominus' (see sources in next note). On his resignation Sutton was pensioned off with £20 a year from the rectory.

Master Christopher Talbot, instituted 1485 (patron King Richard III), died 1493.[30]

Richard Shirburn, B.Cn.L., instituted 1493 (patron George Talbot, 4th Earl of Shrewsbury), died 1500.[31] This canon lawyer, archdeacon of Salop and a pluralist in the diocese of Coventry and Lichfield from the time of Bishop Hales, was a residentiary canon of Lichfield cathedral at the time of his institution to Whitchurch.

George Vernon, instituted 1500 (patron George Talbot, 4th Earl of Shrewsbury), died 1534.[32] Vernon was perhaps the Oxford scholar who, with his brother, was at Magdalen Hall in 1494.

Plate 15 Tomb of Sir John Talbot who founded the Grammar School in 1550

John Talbot, D.D., instituted 1534 (patron George Talbot, 4th Earl of Shrewsbury).[33] Dr. Talbot was an illegitimate member of the Talbot family, several of whom mentioned him in their wills. Ordained priest in 1499, he was dead by January 1550, shortly before the opening of Whitchurch grammar school, which he founded with a personal endowment of £200. His monument, with effigy, is in the church opposite that of his ancestor, the 1st Earl of Shrewsbury.

James Nitzens, instituted 1571.[34]

Thomas Mawdesley, D.D., instituted 1585.[35]

James Brookes, instituted 1589.[36] He may be James Gourde *alias* Brookes, M.A. 1579.

Thomas Singleton, D.D., instituted 1606.[37] Originally a Cambridge man and inclined to Puritanism (unhappy with Oxford's defence of clerical non-residency in the 1603 *Answere* to the millenary petition), Dr. Singleton was probably a conformist by the time of his institution to Whitchurch; he was principal of Brasenose College, Oxford, 1595–1614, vice-chancellor of Oxford university 1598–9 and 1611–14, canon of St. Paul's cathedral 1597–1614, canon of Hereford cathedral 1604–14, etc. He died in 1614 and was buried in the university church of St. Mary the Virgin, Oxford. He was presumably a largely absentee rector, and on 14 October 1612 the glebe terrier was signed by Anthony Buckley, 'minister'.[38]

John Rawlinson, D.D., instituted 1614 (patron Sir Thomas Egerton, 1st Baron Ellesmere), died 1631.[39] Dr. Rawlinson was a chaplain to Lord Chancellor Ellesmere (elected chancellor of the university of Oxford in 1610) and William Laud's unsuccessful rival for the presidency of St. John's College, Oxford; after that defeat he became principal of St. Edmund Hall, 1610–31; he was a chaplain to King James I. He died 3 Feb. 1631 and was buried in the chancel at Whitchurch.

Thomas Fowler, M.A., instituted 1631 (patron Alice, Dowager Countess of Derby).[40] Educated at Oxford (Trinity College, later Christ Church), matriculating in 1616, Fowler (D.D. 1643) was the second son of Walter Fowler, of Pendeford (in Tettenhall, Staffs.). He was tutor to Viscount Brackley (2nd Earl of Bridgwater 1649), but after Whitchurch was taken by Sir William Brereton in 1643 he lost his living for refusing to take the Covenant. He seems then to have retired to the Egertons' estate at Little Gaddesden (Herts.), where he died in 1653. His brother Matthew, fifteen years younger, was rector from 1666.[41] The patron (*née* Spencer) was the widow of Lord Chancellor Ellesmere (created Viscount Brackley 1616, d.1617) and relict of the 5th Earl of Derby (d.1594).

Thomas Porter, M.A., occurs perhaps soon after May 1643, ejected 1660.[42] Porter matriculated at Christ's College, Cambridge, in 1616 (M.A. 1623) and was ordained priest in 1623. He became vicar of Hanmer (Flints.) in 1626 and was preacher at St. Catherine Cree, London. It is said that Oliver Cromwell — who matriculated at Cambridge in the same year as Porter[43] — 'thrust' him into Thomas Fowler's cure after Sir William Brereton's taking of Whitchurch in May 1643. Porter was highly regarded by Richard Baxter as 'an ancient, grave Divine of great integrity, blamelessness and Diligence' and an 'excellent' preacher. He became a leader of the Fourth Shropshire (or Whitchurch) Presbyterian Classis established in 1646. It was perhaps during Porter's incumbency that his son and namesake (Christ's College, M.A. 1655) was preacher at Tilstock. Had the Restoration produced a comprehensive Church of England (such as Baxter strove for at the Savoy Conference in 1661), Porter might have become a bishop. In the event, however, although Porter had been episcopally ordained, and although no (pre-war) rival claimant to the living survived, he was ejected well before many Presbyterian ministers were forced out of their benefices under the 1662 Act of Uniformity. Perhaps the patron was responsible for Porter's precipitate ejection, for Bridgwater, a loyalist in the Civil War, had been close to Archbishop Laud and may have disliked Porter's prominent part in Presbyterian ordinations during the Interregnum. (At the Restoration Bridgwater became a protégé of Clarendon and was to take a prominent part, with Clarendon and Bishop Sheldon of London, in managing the conference between Lords and Commons on the Bill that was to become the Act of Uniformity.) After leaving Whitchurch Porter evidently lived in Shrewsbury, where he died in 1667.

Nicholas Bernard, D.D., instituted 1660 (patron John Egerton, 2nd Earl of Bridgwater), died 1661.[44] Bernard was educated at Cambridge and ordained in Ireland in 1626 by Archbishop Ussher of Armagh, whose chaplain he became and from whom he obtained his early preferment. In 1648 he was committed to the Fleet prison, London, for undertaking to preach without the licence of Parliament. Despite this he prospered in England in the 1650s, becoming preacher of Gray's Inn in 1651 and chaplain and almoner to Oliver Cromwell. The funeral sermon that he preached at Ussher's funeral (1656) in Westminster Abbey, when it was published, involved Bernard in controversy with Dr. Peter Heylin, who considered himself to have been slandered. At the Restoration Bernard, who had meanwhile worked hard to give Ussher's literary remains a more royalist and episcopal slant, declined reappointment to his old deanery of Ardagh cathedral; by then old, he 'preferred the learned leisure of a not over-burdensome post' and accepted the rectory of Whitchurch, whence he published a final work on monarchy and church government.[45] He died 15 Oct., and was buried at Whitchurch 7 Nov., 1661.[46]

Richard Heylin, D.D., instituted 1662 (patron John Egerton, 2nd Earl of Bridgwater).[47] Dr. Heylin, a Shropshire man, matriculated at Christ Church in 1616 and was thus an exact Oxford contemporary of the eminent Laudian divine Dr. Peter Heylin (of Magdalen College). He became a canon of Christ Church in 1666 and may then have resigned Whitchurch rectory; he died in 1669.

Matthew Fowler, D.D., instituted 1666 (patron John Egerton, 2nd Earl of Bridgwater).[48] Dr. Fowler was one of the Fowlers of Pendeford (Staffs.) and younger brother of Thomas Fowler, rector from 1631. A fulsome memorial in Latin, commissioned by his widow Letitia, survived the collapse of the medieval church in 1711 and is now at the west end of the north aisle. It tells of his dedication to the monarchy in the troubled times of the Civil War and says that he died 'worn out by care and sleeplessness'.

Clement Sankey, D.D., instituted 1684 (patron John Egerton, 2nd Earl of Bridgwater).[49] He was rector of Settrington (Yorks. E.R.) 1667 and a canon of York 1669–1707. His collection of over 2,000 books forms the basis of the Whitchurch parish library, now deposited in Shropshire Archives.

Plate 16 The church which collapsed in 1711 (drawn by J. North from a picture in the vestry)

Peter Leigh, M.A., instituted 1707 (patrons Jane, Dowager Countess of Bridgwater, and Scroop Egerton, 4th Earl [later 1st Duke] of Bridgwater).[50] Son of Thomas Leigh, of High Leigh (Ches.), Peter Leigh was early preferred to a family benefice — a moiety of Lymm (Ches.), of which he was rector *c*.1689–90. Later (1697) he became vicar of Great Budworth (Ches.) in the patronage of the dean and chapter of Chester. His marriage to a niece of John, 3rd Earl of Bridgwater (d.1701), must have brought him the rich living of Whitchurch: in 1707 his patrons were his wife's aunt and her cousin. The connexion proved profitable to further generations of Leighs, who enjoyed the good living of Myddle 1746–59 — also in the patronage of their kinsmen the Dukes of Bridgwater. It was in Peter Leigh's time at Whitchurch that the new church was built. It was consecrated on 8 October 1713.

The Hon. Henry Egerton, D.C.L., instituted 1720 (patron Scroop Egerton, 1st Duke of Bridgwater).[51] Son of John Egerton, 3rd Earl of Bridgwater, Dr. Egerton was also a canon of Christ Church, Oxford, rector of Myddle 1720–46, clerk of the Closet to King George II, and Bishop of Hereford 1723–46. He and his wife, Lady Elizabeth Adriana (daughter of Hans Willem Bentinck, Earl of Portland), had four children, one of whom (John) was successively Bishop of Bangor (1756–68), of Lichfield and Coventry (1768–71), and of Durham (1771–87).

Richard Newcome, D.D., instituted 1746 (patron John Egerton, 2nd Duke of Bridgwater).[52] Dr. Newcome, of Queens' College, Cambridge, owed his initial preferment to his connexion with the family school in Hackney, 'the largest and most fashionable of all 18th-century private schools'. The father of a pupil there gave him the vicarage of Hursley, Hants, where he took as pupils the Marquesses of Brackley and Hartington. He travelled on the Continent with Lord Brackley in 1744–5 and his father gave him Whitchurch rectory. Through the influence of Lord Hartington's father, the Duke of Devonshire, he was made chaplain to the king, a canon of Windsor (1749–55), and Bishop of Llandaff (1755–61). He was promoted Bishop of St. Asaph in 1761. He gave prebends in each of his cathedrals to his relative Peter Newcome, the antiquary. By 1769 Bishop Newcome had a town house at 72 Dean Street, Soho, but he died at Bath that year after having suffered much from 'the excruciating complaint of the stone'. In 1749 he built the new Rectory, his usual residence while he was Bishop of St. Asaph.

Henry Egerton, M.A., instituted 1770 (patron Francis Egerton, 3rd Duke of Bridgwater).[53] Egerton, son of Henry Egerton, Bishop of Hereford (and rector 1720–46: above), matriculated at Oriel College, Oxford, in 1746 (B.A. 1749, M.A. 1752). He was also a prebendary of Durham Cathedral — preferment owed to his brother, the Bishop of Durham.

James Hallifax, D.D., instituted 1777 (patron Francis Egerton, 3rd Duke of Bridgwater).[54]

Francis Henry Egerton, M.A., F.R.S., instituted 1781 (patron Francis Egerton, 3rd Duke of Bridgwater).[55] This eccentric scholar succeeded as 8th (and last) Earl of Bridgwater in 1823; son of John Egerton, Bishop of Durham (and thus nephew of Henry Egerton, rector 1770–7: above), he enjoyed a valuable prebend in Durham Cathedral. He lived most of his later life in Paris,

Plate 17 Robert Ballard Long, one of Wellington's generals, cousin to Charles Maitland Long. (Source: T.H. McGuffie, ed., Peninsular Cavalry General [1811–13])

Plate 18 Edward Noel Long (1788–1809) friend of Byron and second cousin to Charles Maitland Long. (Source: Byron Society Journal, [1982])

though retaining his valuable rectories of Whitchurch and Myddle (instituted 1797) until he died, unmarried, in 1829. See Chapter Four for more information about him.

Edward Tatham, D.D., instituted 1829 (patron the Dowager Countess of Bridgwater).[56] Dr. Tatham, a Yorshireman educated at Cambridge, was rector of Lincoln College, Oxford, from 1792 until his death in 1834, having been a fellow of the college since 1781; he delivered the Bampton Lectures in 1789. Tatham contributed to architectural alterations to his college, but the college did not prosper under him. Known as a controversialist, he preached a university sermon of some notoriety *c.*1802, and in the university he became an isolated figure as the principal, immoderate, antagonist of Dean Jackson of Christ Church over Oxford's modestly reforming examination statute of 1807. At Whitchurch his incumbency was short, and during those last years of his life he resided mainly at Combe (Bucks.) and was little seen in Oxford (except when he brought his pigs to market), let alone Whitchurch.

Charles Maitland Long, M.A., instituted 1834 (patron the Dowager Countess of Bridgwater).[57] Long (born 1803) was the second son of Samuel Long, of Carshalton Park (Surrey), and his wife Lady Jane, *née* Maitland, daughter of the 7th Earl of Lauderdale; his aunt (by marriage) Amelia, Lady Farnborough (1762–1837), was a granddaughter of John Egerton, Bishop of Durham, and thus a niece of the 7th and 8th Earls of Bridgwater. In 1846 Long was given another of Lord Brownlow's livings, the rectory of Settrington (Yorks. E.R.), worth £1,054 a year *c.*1870; there he remained until his death in 1875. He was Archdeacon of the East Riding 1854–73. Maitland's ancestry included Edward Long, chief judge of the Vice-Admiralty Court of Jamaica. The Longs' association with Jamaica went back to 1655, when it was first occupied, and they became part of the island's governing sugar planters and slave-owning elite. Edward Long made an advantageous marriage with Mary Beckford, whose family

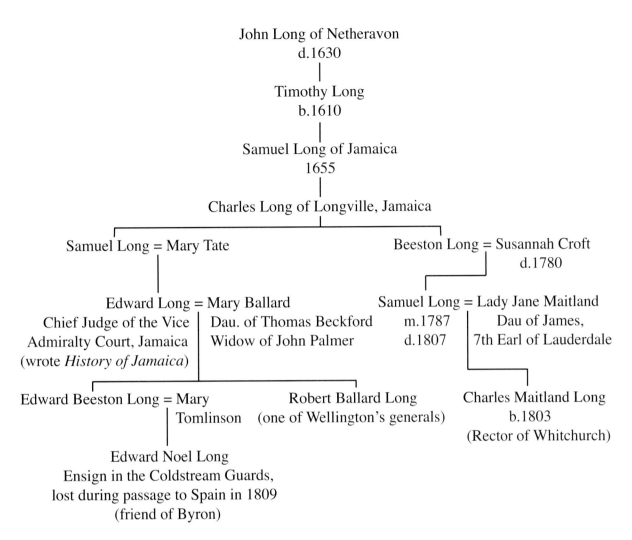

John Long of Netheravon
d.1630

Timothy Long
b.1610

Samuel Long of Jamaica
1655

Charles Long of Longville, Jamaica

Samuel Long = Mary Tate

Beeston Long = Susannah Croft
d.1780

Edward Long = Mary Ballard
Chief Judge of the Vice | Dau. of Thomas Beckford
Admiralty Court, Jamaica | Widow of John Palmer
(wrote *History of Jamaica*)

Samuel Long = Lady Jane Maitland
m.1787 | Dau of James,
d.1807 | 7th Earl of Lauderdale

Edward Beeston Long = Mary
Tomlinson

Robert Ballard Long
(one of Wellington's generals)

Charles Maitland Long
b.1803
(Rector of Whitchurch)

Edward Noel Long
Ensign in the Coldstream Guards,
lost during passage to Spain in 1809
(friend of Byron)

Simplified pedigree of the Long family

owned c.44,670 acres in Jamaica in 1750, but perhaps his greatest claim to fame was his author-ship of the three-volume *History of Jamaica* (1774). Edward's second son, Robert Ballard Long, became a general in the Duke of Wellington's army, and his grandson, Edward Noel Long, Coldstream Guards, was a friend of the poet Lord Byron. Edward was lost at sea in 1809 *en route* for Spain and the Peninsular War. This list of Long luminaries may be brought up to date with the inclusion of Dr. Daniel Miles, a leading dendrochronologist who has worked extensively in Shropshire.

William Henry Egerton, M.A., instituted 1846 (patron the Dowager Countess of Bridgwater).[58] Fourth son of the Revd. Sir Philip Grey-Egerton, Bt., of Malpas, and so a very distant kinsman of the patron. Egerton, rector for 62 years, was born in 1811 and died in 1910. (Portraits of him in youth and old age hang in the vestry and are reproduced here as Plates 19 and 11.) He graduated at Brasenose College, Oxford, and married Louise, daughter of Brooke Cunliffe, by whom he had

*Plate 19 (left) William Henry Egerton
(from a portrait in the vestry)
Plate 20 (above) The Lady Chapel: crest and
inscription to William Henry Egerton*

four sons and two daughters. In 1893 his youngest daughter, Mabel, became the 2nd wife of Robert Peel Ethelston, of Hinton Hall, Whitchurch. It was during Egerton's incumbency that the clock was installed in the church tower in 1849; it is still wound by hand. Thomas Joyce & Sons, of Whitchurch, world-famous for their clocks and a major employer in the town, though now merged with another firm, still deal with the manufacture of tower clocks and the maintenance of old ones from their premises in Station Road. The Lady Chapel, formerly known as the Egerton Chapel (its entrance surmounted by the Egerton crest), was constructed as a memorial to W.H. Egerton. It was designed by the London architect Sir Charles Nicholson.

W.H. Egerton's brother, George Henry Egerton, M.A., was rector of Myddle 1847–1905, a living in which he succeeded Thomas Egerton (son of Wilbraham Egerton, of Tatton, Ches.), rector 1844–7. Lady Bridgwater's presentation of very distantly related Egertons to her livings may suggest family feeling aroused by the imminent extinction of the Bridgwater line.

Sydney Dugdale, M.A., instituted 1909 (patron 3rd Earl Brownlow).[59] The Dugdales were a Lancashire family, whose elder line had settled at Wroxall Abbey (Warws.) in 1861.[60] Sydney Dugdale's father, John Dugdale, high sheriff of Montgomeryshire 1863, was a younger son and seated at Llwyn, a fine early 18th-century house[61] near Llanfyllin (Mont.); Sydney was his fourth son. Llwyn descended to the eldest son in 1903. From the 1890s to *c*.1930 the second son Walter, a Shropshire magistrate (and father of Lt.-Col. W.G. Dugdale, a county councillor), lived at Meeson Hall near Wellington,[62] and the third son Charles Tertius lived at Terrick Hall, Whitchurch;[63] a fifth son lived at Rowney Priory, Ware (Herts.). Sydney Dugdale's eldest sister Mary married the prominent Lancashire gentleman and magistrate Thomas Fenwick Fenwick (d.1907), of Burrow Hall, where she long survived him.[64] Dugdale's daughter married H.H. Hardy, headmaster of

Cheltenham College 1919–32 and of Shrewsbury School 1932–44.[65] Dugdale, a prebendary of Hereford cathedral, had no parochial cure after he left Whitchurch to live at Aston Hall, Aston-on-Clun, where he long survived — dying during the Second World War.[66]

Hugh Hanmer, M.A., instituted 1920 (patron 3rd Earl Brownlow).[67] Sixth son of the Revd. Henry Hanmer (and so nephew of Sir John Hanmer, of Bettisfield Park, Flintshire, 3rd Bt.; created Lord Hanmer 1872), he was also brother-in-law of Edmund Ethelston, of Hinton Hall, Whitchurch. At the outset of his career Hanmer was vicar of Hanmer (Flints.) 1891–8; he was rural dean of Whitchurch 1926–7, rector of Selattyn 1927–31, and rural dean of Oswestry 1927–34. He died at Oswestry in 1939. He was the last rector to live in the Old Rectory.

William Charles Griffith, M.A., instituted 1927 (patron Baron Brownlow).[68] He had previously (1921–7) been rector of Belton (Lincs.), the parish church of Lord Brownlow's seat, Belton House, near Grantham.

Plate 21 The institution of David Jenkins in 1973.
Left to right: Arthur Windsor (churchwarden), Archdeacon Austerberry (front), Basil Mawson (rural dean and rector of Wem), David Jenkins, Bishop Stretton Reeves (bishop of Lichfield), Henry Richards, Raymond Davies (curate and bishop's chaplain for the day), Sidney Latham (churchwarden)

John Henry Hall, M.A., instituted 1938 (patron 6th Baron Brownlow). He was formerly Vicar of Shifnal and greatly concerned with the armed forces, serving as Senior Chaplain to the Forces and Deputy Assistant Chaplain General throughout the war. He had been awarded a Territorial Decoration in 1941 and was appointed Honorary Chaplain to the Forces in 1945. He was a Prebend of Dasset Parva in Lichfield Cathedral between 1960 and 1963.[69]

Charles Arthur Chamberlain, B.A., instituted 1964 (patron 6th Baron Brownlow). He served with an emergency commission as Chaplain to the Forces during the war. Before coming to Whitchurch he was vicar of Tonge and of Bushbury.[70]

Richard David Jenkins, M.A., instituted 1973 (patron 6th Baron Brownlow).[71] David Jenkins was ordained priest in 1962, served curacies in the dioceses of Derby and Durham 1961–8 and was vicar of Walsall, Pleck and Bescott 1968–73. He was rural dean of Wem and Whitchurch 1985–95, priest in charge of Tilstock and Whixall 1992–5, and prebendary of Gaia Major in Lichfield Cathedral 1993–7; in 1997 he retired with his wife, Grace, to the Council House, Shrewsbury. The Jenkinses' years in Whitchurch are fondly remembered and this book is dedicated to them in acknowledgement.

Andrew Roy Ridley, B.A., instituted 1998 (patron the Bishop of Lichfield).[72] He served in Chester diocese 1979–98, was ordained priest in 1980 and was rural dean of Wem and Whitchurch from 2001.

RECTORAMA

In 1996 the verger at St. Alkmund's, Pauline Stokes, noticed that 1996 marked the 700th anniversary of the first recorded Rector of Whitchurch, James Fraunceys, mentioned in 1296. A celebration was called for and David's many friends and devoted parishioners helped him to stage a pageant with narration and music in the church, and there was also an exhibition and a performance of 'Rectorious', the story told by tableaux and music with the players in full costume. National events were linked to local history, David himself taking the part of Henry VIII, and to the buildings of the church and the rectory. The late Stanley North and his wife Jean, the co-author of this

Plate 22a The rector in front of the Norman church

book, produced a remarkable set of drawings for display and these are included here. The figures and the costumes are, of, course, drawn from imagination, but that of Sir John Talbot, who founded the Grammar School, is based on his effigy in the church. Observing a likeness between the known portrait of the eccentric Francis Henry Egerton and Randolph Caldicott's 'Great Panjandrum', Jean took the liberty of substituting the Rev. Egerton for the great she-bear in Caldicott's well-known depiction of Whitchurch High Street in the Panjandrum series.

Plate 22b *Fifteenth-century rector standing by Whitchurch castle, with the church beyond*

Plate 22c *The rector John Talbot founded the grammar school*

Plate 22d *The Rev. Matthew Fowler preaching in the medieval church*

Plate 22e *The Rev. Peter Leigh by the newly-built church*

Plate 22g The Rev. William Henry Egerton
sitting in the garden by the Rectory

Plate 22f The Rev. Francis Henry Egerton
(with apologies to Randolph Caldecott)

8 WARTIME AT THE OLD RECTORY: THE 'Y' STATION

ORIGINS

At the start of the Second World War in 1939 many large houses throughout Britain were requisitioned by the government for various uses by the services. This power, which still exists, dates back to the Defence Act of 1842. Several large houses in and around Whitchurch became billets and the Old Rectory was taken over to become a top secret establishment listening into and receiving messages that were being transmitted both by the enemy and the diplomatic traffic between various neutral countries. Before describing what took place it is necessary to outline the history of wireless intelligence or 'Y' as it became called. Only by understanding the background can the work that went on at the old Rectory be appreciated, and why an air of secrecy still pervades the place. All who worked there were bound by the Official Secrets Act, and to allay local curiosity the rumour was circulated that it was a Radar station.

The foundations of wireless or radio telegraphy were laid by the theoretical work of James Clerk Maxwell in 1871 and the experimental research of Heinrich Rudolph Hertz who discovered electro-magnetic waves. Guglielmo Marconi, expanding on this research, found that it was possible to convert electro-magnetic waves into electricity, and in 1895 he constructed an apparatus capable of sending, amplifying and receiving wireless signals. The Italian court showed little interest and Marconi was advised to take his invention to London, then the centre of the maritime world.

Following experiments in Britain, the General Post Office (GPO), the Royal Navy and to a lesser degree the Army became interested and could see the potential for sending messages through the air without cables. For the previous twenty years or so the GPO had had a monopoly of electrical telegraphy and was able to transmit by Morse code messages at a speed of up to 400 words per minute along its land lines and under the sea by submarine cable. With the help of the GPO, Marconi was able to develop his system and the Wireless Telegraphy & Signal Co., formed in 1897, built the first station in the Isle of Wight. This sent a signal from a 120ft. aerial to a steamer sailing between Swanage and the Isle of Wight.[1]

The Admiralty realised that this could be used for transmission from ship-to-ship and ship-to-shore for which telegraphy by cable was useless. The first message across the Atlantic was transmitted in 1902 between Poldhu in Cornwall and Canada.[2]

During the Boer War (1899–1902) the Army had little success with wireless and continued to lay land lines for communication, but the Royal Navy established two shore stations in South Africa which proved successful. Six Marconi shore stations in England and Ireland were ordered and wireless equipment was installed on twenty-six warships. A unit called 'Section H' was set up with the assistance of the Metropolitan Police to monitor and censor mail and cables resulting in the accumulation of useful intelligence.[3]

By this time other European countries had become interested in the science, and at an international conference held in Berlin in 1903, all countries, with the exception of Britain and Italy, agreed to pool their technical information. Germany in particular had been researching long-distance wireless.

The Committee of Imperial Defence (CID) was formed after the Boer War to co-ordinate service strategy and to review Britain's intelligence capacity. This led to the formation of a secret service bureau which was later to be called MI5. Meanwhile Marconi was proposing an Imperial Wireless Chain, an impressive scheme to link England with about twenty places in its far-flung empire. The CID eventually allowed six stations to be built linking England with Australia.[4]

People generally were now becoming aware of wireless telegraphy, and the press were not slow to take advantage. This was highlighted in 1910 by the famous case of Dr. Crippen, the murderer, being apprehended in Quebec after the captain of the *Montrose* on which Crippen and his disguised lover were escaping, had recognized the doctor and sent his description by wireless to Scotland Yard. A detective was despatched by a fast boat and was able to arrest Crippen as he stepped ashore. Not only was this a demonstration of the use of wireless telegraphy but it also highlighted the possibility of interception as several London newspapers had listened into the messages between the Montrose and the police and had printed the story in their next editions.[5]

Prior to the outbreak of the First World War (1914–18), the Naval Intelligence Division (NID) together with the Marconi company had made a comprehensive survey of all the wireless stations both at home and abroad showing the exact stage of wireless development worldwide and had categorised those which had a military purpose. In Britain, apart from the GPO, naval stations and Marconi commercial stations, there were, by this time, many amateurs called 'radio hams' operating home-made 'cats' whisker' sets. When war came Defence Regulations required all sets to be surrendered, but the amateurs felt that they could assist in the war effort, and after much persuasion, a select group were enrolled as Special Constables and sworn to secrecy. The ban remained on all others. The government was aware that wireless might be used for espionage and by September 1914 forty-four stations had been set up to monitor transmissions. All external cables were channelled through centres administered by the GPO responsible to the War Office, and had total control over information leaving the U.K. The censorship of radio telegraphy was left to the Navy and all transmissions were checked at the Old Admiralty. Many commercial firms were now communicating by wireless and sending messages in their own cipher. They were now obliged to use plain English, although a few firms came to an agreement to continue by providing the Board of Trade with a copy of their own code.[6]

Unlike the Navy, the Army was still reluctant to depend on wireless, though the British cavalry in France were given some sets. However, some near the front lines had picked up signals from the German lines and it was realised that interception could give much information. In 1915 Marconi was directed to send technicians with a wireless compass to put together a Direction Finding (DF) unit. They set up aerials at Blendeques and Abbeville and when the results were compared with the contents of the intercepted messages it was possible to identify German units and plot their movements. This was the birth of modern Signals Intelligence (SIGINT).[7]

At home a small network of DF stations were built linked to the War Office to intercept signals from zeppelins, and eventually another network of high-masted directional aerials were erected along the east coast from the Shetlands to Westgate-on-Sea and linked to the Admiralty. By 1916 a number of academics had been drafted into the Intelligence Corps to study the intercepts and develop the science of traffic analysis, and a Decryption Unit was initiated to break the enemy's codes.[8]

After the war the various units of SIGINT were incorporated into the Government Code and Cypher School (GC & CS), initially under the control of the Director of Naval Intelligence but eventually the Foreign Office (MI6).

Attention was now turned to monitoring Soviet and Japanese traffic. In 1920 the new Royal Corps of Signals absorbed the old Royal Engineers Signal Service which, overseas, maintained a network of stations known as Army Chain. All reports were relayed to GC & CS which was responsible for cryptanalysis; the Army and Navy keeping responsibility, respectively, for monitoring traffic analysis. The 'Y' Committee was formed in 1928 to co-ordinate the work of the various service intercept stations. Sarafand in Palestine was a major centre and they were also established in Shanghai and on the north-west frontier of India and Burma. By 1934 the Royal Air Force became interested in foreign wireless signals and established a small unit to monitor traffic at RAF Waddington, near Lincoln.[9]

The British Broadcasting Company (later Corporation) had been created in 1922 and was broadcasting music and news items to cat's whisker sets. These progressed to single-valve sets powered by 2-volt accumulators which could be recharged at local radio shops and garages, and then to more expensive 120-volt battery operated sets. These were very popular and many homes could boast a set of some sort by the late 1920s. Many young men built their own sets and found that not only could they listen to the BBC but could also send messages to their like-minded friends.

DEVELOPMENT

Until 1937 the main preoccupation had been with Soviet and Japanese traffic but during the Spanish Civil War there was a great deal of wireless traffic between Spain, Germany and Italy. Interception was conducted chiefly from the War Office at Fort Bridgewoods, a fort that had been built in 1883 to protect the naval town of Chatham, and at Flowerdown, the Admiralty station near Winchester. About this time the 'Y' Committee arranged for three new GPO stations to be prepared at Sandridge, near St. Albans, Cupar in Fife and Brora in Sutherland; their role would be to concentrate on German and Italian diplomatic traffic. Sandridge was to become operational in September 1939.[10]

The Spanish Civil War was the first opportunity to intercept and analyse Enigma based traffic. Enigma was an automatic electro-magnetic ciphering machine which was widely available on the continent and used commercially by banks and other organisations to encode their messages (pls. 23 and 24, fig. 46). In 1926 the Germans began working on a military version with which they equipped their army, navy and air-force. The Admiralty had purchased two of the commercial machines in 1928 and eventually, after eight years of consideration, the British government decided that the Air Ministry should supervise the construction of a similar cipher machine. This

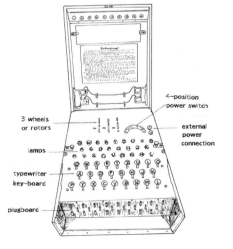

3 wheels
or rotors

lamps

typewriter
key–board

plugboard

4–position
power switch

external
power
connection

*Plate 23 (top left) The 3-rotor Enigma machine
as was used by the German Luftwaffe and Army.
The front of the case is open to show the* Steckerboard

Figure 46 (left) Key to the Enigma machine

*Plate 24 (top right) The Enigma machine
with the inner lid raised to show the 3 rotors
and the bulb array*

was manufactured by the Creed Teleprinter Co. and called the TypeX. It gradually became available to the RAF and the War Office. It was believed that both TypeX and Enigma were impenetrable if used correctly and that it was only by making use of cribs and exploiting human error that the codes could be broken. The Poles had been intercepting German traffic early on the 1930s and had also built their own Enigma machine which had enabled them to identify some of the keys used by the Germans. The Poles were much more advanced than the British and had developed a contraption which they called a 'Bombe', a decoding device which, at high speed, could try thousands of permutations to discover a key. Just before the war began they made one of their Enigma machines and details of their bombe available to the British. There had also been some collaboration with France and a jointly-run intercept station had been set up in the south of France to monitor Italian naval and air-force traffic.[11]

Seigfried Maruhn, a signal operator in the Tenth Panzer Army Signal Regiment describes how the Enigma machine was operated.[12]

> Actually it is not very difficult to use. The trickiest part is setting the initial conditions of the machine. One had to follow the instructions laid down in a master plan, issued monthly. There were five wheels (*walzen*) from which to choose; three were inserted in the prescribed order. On each wheel a rotary ring had to be turned to a given position, then a number of cables had to be switched on at the front of the machine to connect pairs of letters. These initial conditions had to be established on both sides, sender and receiver. After all, no message can be safely delivered if sender and receiver have not completely synchronised their machines. The initial setting of the wheels was part of the message itself.
>
> From then on all you had to do was hit the typewriter keys of the Enigma and take down the letters lighting up on the display. Usually we worked in teams of two, one soldier typing, the other jotting down the results. The encoded text, thus acquired, would then be transmitted as Morse code in groups of five. Each message preceded by the Morse code 'ka' (dash dot dash / dot dash), closing individual messages with an 'ar' (dot dash / dot dash dot) and ending the transmission 'sk' (dot dot dot / dash dot dash). We named this last code '*scluss kamerad*', meaning 'end, comrade'.
>
> Receiving and decoding a message was similarly simple. The signalman on duty took down the letters of the message transmitted in Morse code and then, usually with help of another soldier, deciphered the message on the Enigma, reversing the encryption process. He typed the letters of the encrypted message and received plain text. This was taken down on forms and forwarded to the addressee. So for most of us the Enigma machine was just a black box. You put something in at one end and received something else at the other. Input and output were connected in some mysterious way. The Greek name seemed to express this mystery perfectly. I recall that I knew at least the elementary workings of the machine. For example I realised that on the first level the individual letters of the message were converted by the *Steckerverbindungen* of the plug board in the traditional 1:1 way; then the letter just acquired was sent to the first wheel and changed again in a way that depended on the internal wiring of the wheel. This process was repeated twice, further variations being produced by the wheels turning at a prescribed rate. I did not know at the time that there was a reflector at the end, sending the signals back through all three wheels before it finally reached the display.

Plate 25 Bletchley Park, Buckinghamshire — the code-breaking centre

The Germans believed their messages were completely safe. The real danger, they thought, was that a machine, the wheels and a current table of settings would fall into enemy hands, and therefore the operators had strict orders to destroy the machine and tables if capture seemed imminent. They did not realise that a crib could be discovered from the initial and closing parts of the message which always remained the same.

GC and CS began preparing for war. In 1938 a German section had been added and the staff increased. There was a fear that the London headquarters would be a prime target in an attack. They looked for alternative accommodation and a large country house was bought in 1938 at Bletchley Park with enough land for all the huts it was going to require. It was in a good position, on a main railway line and main roads between London and the north and mid-way between Oxford and Cambridge from where many of the 'brains' were to come. During the following year staff were slowly moved from London, though MI6 headquarters remained at 54, Broadway, St. James, and the diplomatic cryptographic department remained in Berkeley Street, London. By August 1939 the main group of a few hundred had been transferred. There is now a well-documented history of war-time Bletchley Park, but suffice it to say here that it became the hub of a giant organisation decoding, analysing and interpreting the information sent to it by outlying intercept stations and became known as the Government Communications Headquarters (GCHQ). By June 1944 the staff numbered 6,812 and included some of the finest brains in the country.

A Metropolitan Police radio station established before the war at Denmark Hill, South London, and that, together with the GPO station at Sandridge, the RAF stations at RAF Waddington and RAF Cheadle, and the War Office station at Fort Bridgewoods now transmitted their intercepts to Bletchley Park. The Royal Navy was already highly organised; twelve high-frequency stations had been built in various world-wide locations and these transmitted to three stations in England: Horsea Island in Portsmouth Harbour, Cleethorpes and Flowerdown. They were also experimenting with a system using low-frequency for sending and receiving signals from underwater submarines.[13]

EXPANSION

Other stations soon followed. Hanslope Park, another large country house near Bletchley Park, became the first major Foreign Office station and Special Communications Unit (SCU). Cupar and Brora in Scotland followed. Directional Finding (DF) stations were set up in Thurso and Forfar in Scotland, Bridgwater in Somerset, Gilnahirk in Northern Ireland, St. Erth in Cornwall, Wymondham in Norfolk and also at Hanslope Park.[14]

Unlike the First World War, this time it was realised that radio amateurs could make a great contribution and a Radio Security Service (RSS) was formed. The amateurs were skilled interceptors as they were accustomed to tune into very weak signals. Initially they were instructed to discover whether any illegal transmissions were being made from this country to the enemy. But in the absence of any such transmissions they developed their own 'Y' station at Arkley near Barnet, Hertfordshire and by the end of the war had established a network of intercept and DF stations. Many amateurs also worked from home and were called Voluntary Interceptors (VIs).[15]

As the threat of invasion grew the three services expanded their interception programmes. Fort Bridgewoods, which was in a vulnerable position in the south-east, was moved to Beaumanor Hall in Leicestershire and became one of the largest intercept stations employing many hundreds of Auxilliary Territorial Service women (ATS). The RAF built new stations at Montrose in Scotland and at Chicksands Priory, Bedfordshire. The SIS (MI6) had leased Whaddon Hall, Buckinghamshire and around it grew a complex network of intercept stations and others where transmissions to and from agents in the field were operated by the Special Operations Executive (SOE). Also in the network were workshops manufacturing special wireless transceivers for use by secret agents and equipment for mobile units.[16]

THE WHITCHURCH CONNECTION

About this time the GPO station at Sandridge was also looking for another site away from possible bombing or worse, so plans were made for a stand-by station far removed from the danger of enemy action.[17] The small market town of Whitchurch in Shropshire, 176 miles north of London and 50 or so miles from any other vital targets, was chosen. The old Rectory was requisitioned in 1941 and became a Post Office Reserve wireless station. It was in a good position on the fringe of the town and in a secluded situation.

The Ministry of Works drew up plans for alterations and additions to the structure.[18] The floors at ground- and first-floor level were strengthened with brick piers and timber baulks in the cellar, toilets for men on the ground floor and women on the first-floor were installed along with a ducting system for fans. External buttresses were built at the rear between the seven ground-floor windows (see fig. 10). The lower halves of these windows were bricked up and ceramic tubes inserted at about six-inch centres. These were of two types, smooth and fluted, and allowed access for the cables from the large array of aerials in the fields to the north and north-east of the house. There were two very tall aerials and many shorter ones; the fluted tubes took cables from the Rhombic directional aerials and the smooth ones took those from the Dipoles.[19]

Internally the cables were connected to the wireless receivers. Most of these were the HRO receivers designed by James Midler and manufactured by the National Radio Company of Masachusettes (fig. 47). The original had been produced as a domestic short-wave receiver in the

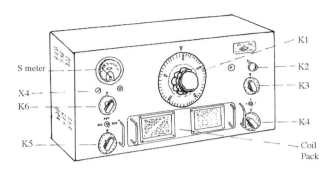

Plate 26 (top left)
The rear of the Old Rectory

Plate 27 (bottom left)
A blocked window with smooth
and fluted tubes for cables

Plate 28 (bottom centre) Some of the
aerials; there were two or three fields full
of them (photo courtesy Mary Rudd)

Plate 29 (bottom right)
G.P.O. Insulator used at the Old Rectory
(photo courtesy W. Moran)

Figure 47 (right)
HRO Communications Receiver

K1 main tuning control for changing receivers

K2 & 3 selectivity control to separate closed spaced code stations

K4 radio frequency gain control

K5 oscillator for use in receiving code with a different pitch or note

K6 volume control for audio level in headphones

X4 on/off switch for signal strength above

COIL PACK which can be pulled out and replaced with another when switching to a different band

1930s, but its potential was realised by the military and over 10,000 sets were in use during the war. It was joked by the manufacturer's work-force that HRO stood for 'helluva rush order'.[20] It was the set preferred by operators as it was considered to be the most sensitive and accurate, and it could be fine-tuned which meant that a drifting station could be followed with the minimum amount of dial movement. Marconi CR100 communication receivers were also used.

Creed Model 7B teleprinters were installed and connected to Bletchley Park by land lines. Upstairs in the Old Rectory there was a workshop for the maintenance engineers and a room with an array of telephones and a switchboard. It was believed by the staff that military uniforms were stored in a small upstairs room for use in the event of invasion and capture.[21] Presumably it was thought that by appearing to be service personnel they would not have been shot. In the cellar a room with the door marked 'CIPHER PLEASE KNOCK AND WAIT' was believed to house a TypeX machine (pl. 30). The main door

Plate 30 The British TypeX rotor machine
(photo courtesy W. Moran)

Plate 31 Door to Cellar
(photo courtesy W. Moran)

Figure 48 Cellar doors and trunking showing wartime 'Y' station use

Plate 32
Stirrup pump in the
cellar, part of the
ARP equipment

at the head of the cellar steps is labelled 'AIR RAID SHELTER' (pl. 31) and two doors in the cellar are marked 'ARP' (Air Raid Precautions) (fig. 48). Dug-out shelters were also in the grounds close to the house (pl. 33). One was very large, over 12ft. wide, and clearly intended to shelter many personnel. There was access to it from the grounds and also from a tunnel leading from the cellar. Blocking brickwork in the north-west corner indicates the access point. Fortunately these provisions were never needed.

The Old Rectory became operative in early 1942 and became part of the 'Y' service which had expanded to more than sixty stations (see map, fig. 49). Sandridge did not need to re-locate and is still operational today. There seems to be no known official record of the exact number of stations established during the war. Possibly there were other small ones similar to Whitchurch, and there were many mobile units which operated both at home and abroad. They were known as 'Home Defence Units' (HDU) 'a title chosen because it sounded no more secret than 'Home Guard'. The choice illustrated a principle of secrecy: if you wish to direct attention from your real purpose adopt a title which sounds boring and inoffensive'.[22]

Staff were drafted in from all parts of the country to run Whitchurch and to the young ladies who were drafted in from 1943 they appeared middle-aged, although anyone over the age of thirty looks middle-aged when one is only eighteen. Some had probably served in the First World War and all of them, it seems, had a GPO telephone, radio or wireless

Plate 33 The underground air raid shelter in 2005

communications background. Three came from radio stations: George Holmes and To
from Humber radio and Tommy Woods from Burnham. It is not known where this old
gent was trained, but Sandridge is a possibility. They were all very proficient by the
year when many young ladies, mostly in their teens, were enrolled. Eight of the origin
ment became supervisors: Edgar Vernon, George Holmes, Tom Tilley, Frank Thor
Woodward, Tommy Woods, Bill Sharrat and, in overall charge, Mr. Thompson wh
been ex-Navy (pls. 34 and 35).[23]

It is apparent from a document supplied to the Canadian National Security E
GCCS on 3 June 1942 that Whitchurch was then intercepting diplomatic traffic
following countries:

Eire – Vatican City
France – Japan, Saigon and Hanoi, Sweden, USA, Romania, Argentina, Bra
    Hungary, Portugal, French Indo-China, Syria, and French Colonies
Japan – Afghanistan
Romania – Germany, Italy
USSR – Belgian Congo, Eire, USA

Erratum
Page 71, Plate 30
'The British TypeX rotor machine' should read 'Creed Model 7B teleprinter'.

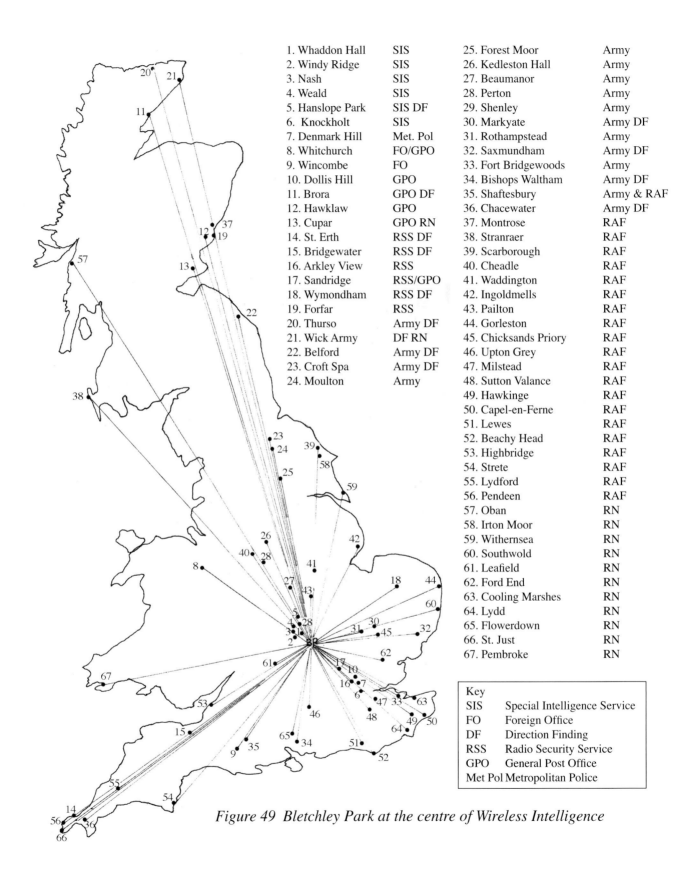

1. Whaddon Hall	SIS	25. Forest Moor	Army
2. Windy Ridge	SIS	26. Kedleston Hall	Army
3. Nash	SIS	27. Beaumanor	Army
4. Weald	SIS	28. Perton	Army
5. Hanslope Park	SIS DF	29. Shenley	Army
6. Knockholt	SIS	30. Markyate	Army DF
7. Denmark Hill	Met. Pol	31. Rothampstead	Army
8. Whitchurch	FO/GPO	32. Saxmundham	Army DF
9. Wincombe	FO	33. Fort Bridgewoods	Army
10. Dollis Hill	GPO	34. Bishops Waltham	Army DF
11. Brora	GPO DF	35. Shaftesbury	Army & RAF
12. Hawklaw	GPO	36. Chacewater	Army DF
13. Cupar	GPO RN	37. Montrose	RAF
14. St. Erth	RSS DF	38. Stranraer	RAF
15. Bridgewater	RSS DF	39. Scarborough	RAF
16. Arkley View	RSS	40. Cheadle	RAF
17. Sandridge	RSS/GPO	41. Waddington	RAF
18. Wymondham	RSS DF	42. Ingoldmells	RAF
19. Forfar	RSS	43. Pailton	RAF
20. Thurso	Army DF	44. Gorleston	RAF
21. Wick Army	DF RN	45. Chicksands Priory	RAF
22. Belford	Army DF	46. Upton Grey	RAF
23. Croft Spa	Army DF	47. Milstead	RAF
24. Moulton	Army	48. Sutton Valance	RAF
		49. Hawkinge	RAF
		50. Capel-en-Ferne	RAF
		51. Lewes	RAF
		52. Beachy Head	RAF
		53. Highbridge	RAF
		54. Strete	RAF
		55. Lydford	RAF
		56. Pendeen	RAF
		57. Oban	RN
		58. Irton Moor	RN
		59. Withernsea	RN
		60. Southwold	RN
		61. Leafield	RN
		62. Ford End	RN
		63. Cooling Marshes	RN
		64. Lydd	RN
		65. Flowerdown	RN
		66. St. Just	RN
		67. Pembroke	RN

Key	
SIS	Special Intelligence Service
FO	Foreign Office
DF	Direction Finding
RSS	Radio Security Service
GPO	General Post Office
Met Pol	Metropolitan Police

Figure 49 Bletchley Park at the centre of Wireless Intelligence

Plate 34 Supervisors at the Old Rectory
From left: Back row: Teddy Vernon, George Holmes, ?, Tom Tilley, Tommy Woods
Front row: Bill Sharratt (second in command), Mr. Thompson (in command), ?, Frank Thorne

The document also included a list of world-wide traffic between many neutral countries which was being intercepted by the other GPO stations: Baldock, Cupar, Sandridge, Brora, St. Alban's and the Metropolitan Police Station at Denmark Hill.[24]

Intercept material was passed daily to the Prime Minister, Winston Churchill, and he was particularly interested in decrypts of diplomatic traffic which he received unedited. This interest had begun in 1915 when he was First Lord of the Admiralty, had continued through the intervening years, and now became vitally important. Churchill depended on these messages as much as on the military information being submitted to him routinely.[25]

The young ladies were recruited from all parts of the country, mostly from the Post Office telephone companies. They were sent for training at the Foreign Office Radio School at Cornwall House near Waterloo station where they learned Morse, touch typing and the intricacies of radio sets, how to tune a set and to search through the various frequencies to locate the message. Each had its own call sign and it was possible to recognise the control station signalling back and forth to the out stations. Directly the control station was located, the information would be sent to Bletchley Park. The Germans changed their frequencies at midnight, so at that time a search would

[Handwritten names on reverse of photograph, partially legible:]

Holmes Humber Radio GKZ
Plymouth Northampton GUMA
Rita Oblade London
A.I. Leir London S.E.D.O.
James S. Barmouth
J. W. Dampott Berkhamsted
Pag. Pelling Manchester (all banks).

Nell Seal. Droylsden so msdre.
E.F. Agutter Coventry Warwicks
N. M. Lloyd (aberystwyth)
F. Walton Middlesbrough
Bill Williams London BBC
M.J. Brown
T. Wood
Mrs Walker

B. Garrison Kirkby Lonsdale (W.R.)
J. Tilly, Humber Radio
Banks
H. Cromack. Doncaster.
M. McKay

Plate 35 'Y' station staff at the Old Rectory. 'Teddy' Vernon (overseer), second from left, back row, together with the names that are recorded on the reverse of the photograph. (Photo supplied by Muriel Vernon, daughter-in-law of Edgar Fisher 'Teddy' Vernon)

Plate 36 Cloverfields, a young ladies hostel in wartime (photo courtesy of W. Moran)

be made to locate them again. It was not until they transferred to Whitchurch that they were trained to listen to both enemy and neutral messages.[26]

Cloverfields, a large house in Chester Road, was requisitioned and became a hostel for the young ladies, the older staff were billeted in private houses around the town. Some were accommodated in Hughes Hotel (now Weston House) in Green End. There were about one hundred working at the Old Rectory, plus engineers who kept everything in working order.

MEMORIES (Extracts from personal communications)

After training in London, about twelve of us were posted to Whitchurch but had to wait some time for Cloverfields to be converted into a hostel to accommodate twenty-eight girls. We were the first young people at the Old Rectory and we caused quite a stir among its more elderly inhabitants. I have many happy memories of the place — the work was hard but interesting, although at the time we were not aware of the importance of what we were doing. We spent long hours day and night searching for enemy radio activity and recording German messages of all descriptions.'[27] (June Briggs, *née* Ibbotson)

I worked in the telephone manager's office in Liverpool and did the training at Cornwall House and was billeted at 8, Fitzroy Square. Two girls were killed when they went to the Guards' chapel for Sunday service. A doodle-bug [flying bomb] scored a direct hit. The rest of us were sent to Whitchurch for further training.[28] (Mary Rudd, *née* Butler)

Our shifts were as follows: 8 am – 5pm; 5 pm –11 pm; 11pm – 8pm. We spent most of the day on receivers, and as stations closed down at night we were then on teleprinters typing out mostly codes which did get a bit tedious. We were later asked if anyone would volunteer to go to the 'Y' station at Brora in north Scotland for a six-month period. It turned out to be almost twelve months and by then we were longing to get back to Whitchurch. We shared the 'baronial hall' with the naval people for our lunches which consisted of Spam sandwiches made up for us at Cloverfields.[29] (Joan Broadhurst)

I worked at the Old Rectory from early 1944 until it closed in 1950, and very interesting and enjoyable it was. My husband was in the ex-forces intake in 1947. My first duties were of a clerical nature, scrutinising and sorting coded and plain language traffic ready for despatch to Station X. Every morning a military style van arrived to take the traffic. A few months later I went to Cornwall House in London to train for a wireless operator. The school was run by the Inland Office of Wireless Telegraphy which I think was a branch of the Post Office. All the instructors were certainly Post Office personnel. I think I was on a rota of mostly men and was very spoiled due to my tender age of seventeen! We worked 8am to 1pm and 8am to 1.30pm and back at 11pm to 8am; also 8am to 5pm and 4.30pm to 11pm. Quite varied at times. We also did a stint in the teleprinter room typing up the traffic to Bletchley Park. Night duty was quite good fun when we were in the slip [high-speed Morse; see below] room typing up the traffic and having a sing-song to keep ourselves awake. There was a team of overseers in charge; Tom Tilley and George Holmes from Humber radio, bluff Yorkshireman Tommy Woods from Burnham radio and my favourite, Georgie Woodward, very eccentric and from Portishead. Oh yes, and Mr. Vernon who used to sit knitting on night duty in the slip room. The whole staff were a very mixed bunch, all ex-Post Office telegraphists, male and female from as far apart as Miss McKay from Skye and Bill Williams from the south-east district of London.[30] (Betty Griffiths, *née* Prodger)

At the Old Rectory wireless receivers had been installed in the large rear room, the room to the left of the hall and in the service wing. The slip room and the teleprinters were upstairs where there was also a rest-room. The kitchen at the end of the service wing was nick-named the 'baronial hall'. The staff worked in shifts throughout the day and night and there would be an overseer in charge of each shift and who could be connected to a DF station when necessary.

Joan Nicholls in her book about Beaumanor 'Y' station writes very descriptively of her time as a wireless operator:

> Intercept work is not only being able to take Morse at speed for a concentrated period, it is having the patience to sit for long periods waiting for the first signs of life when a station has gone silent and being able to spring into activity immediately it transmits; rather like a cat sitting outside a mouse-hole.
>
> The stations covered were never the loud ones sending Morse clear as a bell; they were the faint ones, transmitting with the added hazard of static crackling, bursts of atmospheric interference, loud sounds of jamming equipment sent out by the enemy to ensure the message could not be intercepted, and all coming together in the operator's ears. The message had to be accurate as there was no second chance to take it. The message and logs [log-book entries] had to be carefully written to ensure they were read accurately, even though written at speed. When the enemy changed frequency the operator had to handle her set with equal speed and tune into the changed frequency as quickly as the enemy so as not to lose any of the transmission.
>
> More than one station could be using the same air space and with the addition of static, atmospherics and jamming, that tiny piece of the air-waves could be bedlam. The operator had to be able to recognise first of all the sound of the transmitter. This could be, for example, thin or tinny, or soft and deep; all other transmitters on that station could be ignored. Then the particular sound or rhythm made by the enemy sending Morse would be recognised and followed. It is a little like having tinnitus, the sounds do not go away, but the listener trains his brain to ignore whistles and noises, concentrating on the sounds he wants to hear. The station would not necessarily be loud, more often than not it was faint and continually fading. Sometimes a change of aerial helped to boost the signal.[31]

New Equipment

As the war progressed, messages were also being sent out by high-speed Morse. It was impossible to take down Morse at a speed which was often between 80 and 100 words per minute; the average operator could read between 25 and 30 words per minute. To receive this traffic a Marconi Undulator was attached to the receiver (fig. 50). This had a spool of narrow, approximately half-inch white paper tape, sometimes double-banked, fed through the recorder, and an ink stylus would trace a line activated by the sound of the Morse being transmitted.[32]

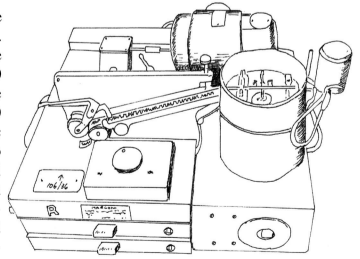

Figure 50 The Marconi Undulator

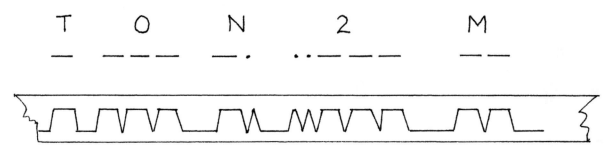

Figure 51 High Speed Slip Morse

The slip or tape, and the sheets with the hand-Morse messages were sent upstairs to the typing room to be translated into 5-block figures for the teleprinter to send to Bletchley Park (Fig. 51). Unlike the staff at the larger 'Y' stations who either operated receivers, teleprinters or typewriters, those at the Old Rectory would be employed in all capacities. The night shifts were mostly occupied in typing up the messages. In addition to them being sent by teleprinter, confirmation of the messages would be collected by despatch riders on motorbicycles or vans, probably on a daily basis. A young boy evacuated from Liverpool called Joe MacDonald, recalled that he delivered newspapers to a large building outside Whitchurch. One day while cycling down the drive he encountered a despatch rider who asked him if he delivered every day and suggested that if he met him at the gate at 8am he would take the papers for him. Whilst the house may not have been the Old Rectory the fact of the young boy remembering cycling down a drive suggests that it was so.[33]

Diplomatic traffic continued to be monitored as the then young ladies can still remember Portugal and Hanoi in particular. The operators, although they knew the source of the messages, had no idea of the content or what happened to it. Everyone in secret work was only informed on a 'need to know' basis. Although they may have felt that they were working in isolation, they were in fact part of a network of many thousands.

Plate 37 Bletchley Park: the gates which admitted despatch riders including those from Whitchurch

BLETCHLEY PARK AND WHITCHURCH

By the 1970s information about Bletchley Park was leaking out and several books were written about the rôle of secret intelligence. Many accounts have since been published and it is now possible to chart the progress of information being sent from the Old Rectory. The messages sent by teleprinter were received in the Registration room and passed to Control, a section which maintained constant contact between the intercept stations and Hut 6 where brilliant mathematicians endeavoured to break the various codes. If the message had been encoded by Enigma, the 'bombe' could help to unravel the intricacies of the daily settings. Alan Turing had built on the design of the Polish 'bombe' and worked out the basic design of an electro-mechanical machine which was manufactured by British Tabulating Machine Co. at Letchworth. Measuring about 6½ft. tall by 7ft. wide and 2½ft. deep it contained a series of thirty (or more as adaptations were made) rotating drums which equated to the wheels of ten (later twelve) Enigma machines. Modifications and improvements followed to allow it to run through all the various possibilities of wheel choice and machine setting at very high speed; it could race through a half-million combinations in a few hours. The operators would wire up the back of the machine to a 'menu' that the code-breakers thought a possibility; this would be a strange pattern of letters and numbers suggesting possible equations of clear letters to enciphered ones. Whenever the machine found a possible match it stopped. The resulting letters would be tried out on a replica Enigma to see if it produced intelligible German text. If that was so the whole text of the message would be decrypted on modified TypeX machines. By the end of the war there were about 2,000 WRNS (Women's Royal Naval Service) operating the many 'bombes' that had been installed in several converted stately homes in Buckinghamshire.[34]

The decoded material was passed to Hut 3 for translation; the information would be analysed, evaluated and categorised as to its urgency or importance. This resulting information (ULTRA) would be sent to the War Office in Whitehall by direct line, and to the Admiralty, Royal Air Force headquarters and other concerns, although the source of the material was always kept secret. If the material was required to be sent to the allied forces it was transmitted by the Special Liaison Unit (SLU) at Whaddon Hall. Here there was a large complex that, apart from its transmitting station at Windy Ridge, had engineering workshops that manufactured wireless transmitting equipment for fitting into various mobile units such as Packard motor cars, Lodge ambulances, small ships and aircraft. These were called Special Communications Units (SCUs). Attached to the commanders in the field of operations and travelling with them, the mobile units, equipped with Whaddon-constructed transmitters and HRO receivers, would receive ULTRA information and pass it to the commander. There were times when the information reached the allied commanders before it reached the enemy commanders, and in the case of the battle of El Alamein it is known to have helped the allied victory over Rommel's Panzer Regiment.

Whaddon also made the sets, called S-phones, which secret agents took into enemy-held lands, and special sets in aircraft to facilitate clear speech communication between the aircraft and the ground agents.[35]

In another Hut was the 'Index'. Every scrap of information coming into Bletchley Park was meticulously sorted and recorded on punch cards and cross-referenced. On request all the relevant information or any particular aspect could be retrieved, and when put together could reveal important facts or pointers; detailed pictures of German military units would emerge.

In addition to Enigma traffic, messages were also being communicated by the enemy on highly sophisticated non-Morse machines. The German manufacturers Lorenz and Siemens had both built cipher-teleprinters; they worked at very high speed and used the International teleprinter or Baudot code. A station at Knockholt in Kent had been established to intercept this traffic on receivers fitted with speed undulators that recorded the messages on punched tape. Bletchley Park called this information FISH. It was very high-grade, sometimes between Hitler and his generals.

Difficulty in deciphering this was eventually overcome by the 'super-bombe' designed by the 'brains' at Bletchley and manufactured by the GPO Reserve station at Dollis Hill, London which became known as COLOSSUS.[36] This traffic was not handled at Whitchurch. COLOSSUS was the forerunner of the modern computer but very large, almost room-sized at first, a far cry from the small lap-top in common use today.

THE NAVAL SECTION AT WHITCHURCH

In 1943 a naval contingent arrived at the Old Rectory. Two Nissen huts were erected in the grounds between the house and the London Road, and the Hollies Hotel became a billet for the sailors. The Hollies had been requisitioned in 1940 for Army use (p. 39).

Geoffrey Rudd transferred to Whitchurch in 1943 from duties in Scapa Flow and was one of the initial five to set up the naval section. Their work was quite separate from the intercept group in the house, and neither group knew exactly what the other was doing. Mr. Elliot (Percy) Mead explains:

> After nearly three years in North Africa and the Middle East I was returned to the UK in about September 1943. I was recalled from leave after three weeks to the Drafting Office at Chatham barracks where I and three others were told we were going to Whitchurch. What type was she? — a frigate, destroyer, minesweeper? No, it was this wireless station in Shropshire. Apparently Whitchurch was a particularly good area for radio reception. So we few sailors found ourselves at Euston and *en route* for Whitchurch, passing through green fields with cows and things.

Plate 38 Naval staff at The Old Rectory in 1944.
Members of the Royal Navy are in uniform, the cooks in white shirts, post office engineers in civilian clothes. (Photo supplied by Mary Rudd)

So we arrived at our new posting. The Hollies was the official Navy HQ and living quarters, and was, for the times, quite comfortable. We were a group of about thirty naval ratings and an equal number of Post Office radio operators, many of the latter having been radio officers in the Merchant Navy.

We were in no way connected with the work going on at the Rectory, although we did know that they were involved with 'Y' reception. The work in our Nissen huts was of a highly specialised kind. One function was to pick up a 'once-off' message from any of the navy ships at sea that had been forced to make a signal in an emergency. To this end there were four operators on one of five radio frequencies so that between the four a complete coded message would be picked up. One Navy and one Post Office operator would be double-banked on each wave. The same went for our sister station at Burnham-on-Sea. This worked very well and it was rarely that we had to ask for a repeat from that ship at sea. We had a secure land line between ourselves and Burnham and to our horror on one occasion we had the Marshalling Yards at Crewe coming over our loudspeakers. It was boring work but very necessary for our lads at sea.

Lieutenant 'Jack' Grossett was the commanding officer when we arrived, and remained with us until just after 'D' day. I forget the name of the next C.O. and only remember the dog. The white ensign flew outside the entrance to the Hollies, and we took turns in lowering the flag at sunset. The dog was always waiting to grab the flag and have a tussle. He would never let go and so we had to drag him to the lawn and swing him round until he dropped off. My Lords of the Admiralty would have had kittens had they known.

Life at the Hollies was very pleasant and so long as we did our work there was little interference from anyone. The night shift from 11pm until 8am was awful but the compensation was free time to do as we liked around town. The morning watch, 8am to noon saw sailors getting out of bed at the last minute, grabbing a sandwich and haring down the back drive of the Hollies, over the Tarporley road, across the fields and slide into their position before 8 o'clock struck. At night many a sailor came to grief falling over a cow in his hurry to get to the station.

When 'D' day, 6 June 1944, came we were standing by to transfer to France as a mobile wireless unit but this fell through, although two or three of our number were sent on this

duty. But we stayed in our Nissen hut until that wonderful day, VE day [8 May 1945]. After partying in the town I arrived back at the Hollies about 2am to be met by a chief petty officer who asked if I was OK as I had to go down on watch and receive reports from U-boats reporting their positions.

We were quite friendly with the Rectory staff, particularly the engineers. We were amazed at the rows and rows of telephone relays they had in their operating unit. The rest of their work was, naturally, very secret.

There was quite an active social life with a mixture of civilian and

Plate 39 The Hollies, requisitioned in 1940

Plate 40 Old Rectory Hockey Team. Joan Broadhurst (who supplied the photo) is on the front left

service men and women. There were dances at the Oddfellows' Hall, and in the hall at the end of the Rectory drive (Church Hall in Claypit Street). Later, when I had a car, we would get as far as Cholmondley Hall dances. We did at times play hockey with the ATS out at Ash. Bikes were the transport of the day and I still recall the magical names of the places we visited: Ellesmere, Malpas, Prees and especially Tilstock. At the Hollies there were two tennis courts at the back which we could use. One of our number, Lofty Whitlam, played for Lincolnshire county. We were allowed to wear civvies and only wore uniform when on duty. This was quite a bonus. So our civvy glad-rags came out and we had to make the most of them until the end of the war when we were kitted out with our 'demob' suits.

Many local friends were made and my particular friends were Betty and Peter Whitfield. They lived at The Park, Tilstock. Being interested in agriculture I spent a lot of time with them. I would go out with them to what were called 'Farm Talks', and visiting various farms discussing techniques. Once on the farm we were clearing out a Dutch barn and we discovered an old car, 1934/5 vintage, three seater, canvas roof, spare wheel and battery on the running board and a dickey seat at the back. This had been known to take ten or eleven Navy and girls to Cholmondley dances. The car belonged to Peter's brother and I used it as a runabout for the rest of my stay.[37]

Burnham-on-Sea remained operational until 1998. Whitchurch is remembered as a very friendly place. There were dances, cinema and sport, particularly hockey and tennis for leisure time activities. Favourite pubs were the Railway Inn and the Horse and Jockey which had many happy sing-song evenings. The Express Café in the High Street, run by the Fulgoni family, was a great favourite for their cakes.

Two further reminiscences from ex-personnel:

We had the Oddfellows' Hall for dancing, though there were often scuffles as the Polish soldiers seemed to be drunk. I played hockey for Whitchurch when we played at the Grammar school, and I also played for Shropshire[38] (Joan Broadhurst)

Sometimes in the evening we would go dancing at the Oddfellows' Hall where Billy Gibbons played, and several American G.I.s showed us the latest dance techniques from the States. Most of us were not too enthusiastic about their attitude to English girls and stopped going. In summer we used our bicycles to explore the countryside and forage for farm eggs and anything else that added to our meagre diet.

Our bicycles took us further afield to Prees Heath and the Witchball Hotel where we cooled off in the swimming pool. We must have cycled many miles touring village public houses where they held collections for the war effort, for example 'Tanks for Victory' week. We had a very good pianist and the local people would come in to have a sing-song and swell the collection boxes. One very cold winter I collected my ice skates from home and skated on the canal at Grindley Brook. We used to walk miles along the banks of the canal in summer'.[39] (June Briggs, *née* Ibbotson)

It would appear that the Oddfellows' Hall did not have a very good reputation, though the exuberance of the off-duty service men is understandable. Naturally, there were many romances and several marriages between the young ladies and the sailors. Mrs. Betty Griffiths writes of her own marriage 'still going strong after fifty-two years'.

Plate 40 Staff at the Old Rectory. This shows the 'watch' in 1944 that included
Mrs. Betty Hayes (née Morris) who is seated in the second row, third from the right.
(Photo supplied by Mrs. Betty Hayes)

VICTORY

The war in Europe ended on 7 May 1945 and the Japanese conflict ended on 14 August, a few days after the dropping of atomic bombs on Hiroshima and Nagasaki. An acknowledgement of the contribution that the 'Y' service had made to the allied victory came from the Director of Bletchley Park:

Memorandum:

YG/143

I have much pleasure in promulgating copies of teleprints from Director Station X and DDY
    1. From Director Station X
    To Scarborough, Flowerdown, Beaumanor, Bishops Waltham, Forest Moor, Shenley, Kedleston Hall, Cheadle, Chicksands, Canterbury, Knockholt, Brora, Denmark Hall, Sandridge, Whitchurch, Wicombe Etousa (for Santa Fe)

    We have fought a long battle together and won; without complete co-operation between us all we could not have accomplished what has been done. On my own behalf and that of the staff at station X I want to thank our comrades in 'Y'. I am able to tell you that as a service we have made a valuable contribution and although this may never be blazoned abroad we can be satisfied that we played our part.

    2. From DDY
    To Beaumanor, Forest Moor, Kedleston Hall, Shenley

    Please pass to all ranks under your command my warmest thanks and congratulations for their magnificent and faithful part in bringing about this day.
        Signed M.J.W. Ellingsworth
        Lt. Col. R. Signals
        O.C. War Office Y Group[40]

It was the end too for Bletchley Park. Winston Churchill, since the time when he was First Lord of the Admiralty at the outbreak of the First World War, had shown a keen interest in Intelligence and particularly in the work of Britain's code-breakers. On a visit in September 1941 the Prime Minister is reported to have likened Bletchley Park to the geese that laid the golden eggs and never cackled. Some authorities have it that he thanked the chickens for laying so well without clucking. Whatever he said, no doubt it was on the lines that if Bletchley Park was the geese/chickens then the 'Y' stations were the farmers who fed and nurtured them.

In June 1946 GCHQ moved from Bletchley Park to Eastcote near Pinner in Middlesex taking two of the Colossus computers and fifty 'bombes', the latter being in use immediately, presumably for decoding Soviet traffic. All the rest is believed to have been destroyed. Later in 1952 another move was made to Cheltenham, where it remains.[41]

AFTER THE WAR

At the Old Rectory work continued. Mrs. Betty Hayes remembers the interception of many messages 'en clair' when USA servicemen were sending messages home. All were recorded and transmitted to Bletchley Park and later to Eastcote. Gradually the staff drifted away to their peace-time occupations, but between 1945 and 1950 when the station finally closed there was an intake of ex-servicemen who came for training in wireless telegraphy and especially in Morse slip-reading. Mrs. June Briggs stayed at the Old Rectory until it closed, and she was one of the last to depart. She moved to Sandridge near St. Albans where, she says, 'we continued working in a more

Plate 41 Set room 'n' in 2004. The windows still show provision for the cables

Plate 42 The hall in 2004. The tin boxes contained the secret wireless sets

modern setting and in a warm and comfortable building'. She was not aware that Whitchurch had been prepared as a reserve station for Sandridge which is still operational today.

Mr. J.D. Evans was one of the ex-servicemen who came to the Old Rectory in the post-war era and he writes:

Although being a Shropshire lad I knew nothing of it until asked at the selection board for the Post Office Radio Service if I knew Whitchurch, I replied that it was only twenty miles from my home village of Crickheath. The central training school at Bletchley Park was full and so on the 2 December 1946 along with the snow which lasted until March/April 1947 I arrived at Brook Farm, Chester Road where I was to be billeted and treated to the best meal I had had for many years. (Mrs. Weston was noted for being a very good cook). Then onto the 'Old Rec.' to join five other recruits and placed in the care of a host of young and not so young ladies. We were ex-Navy with little or no knowledge of the 'Y' service or the part it played in supporting the war effort. The role of the Royal Navy in this was not really clear to us but they departed soon after we arrived. Although we were fully trained radio operators at various levels of competence in RN and RAF requirements, we now had to get to grips with the needs of our new masters; this included touch typing, operating teleprinters and procedures of many different modes. Our main tutor was a dear white-haired lady aptly named Miss Snowdon. Although Morse code receiving and transmitting was our main 'stock-in-trade' its usage was somewhat different from the RN signals requirements.

After a few weeks it became evident that the training had a limited scope; therefore specialist training would follow at different sites. As one of the objectives was to release the young ladies to resume their normal Post Office duties, we gradually took their places. Their departure, though sad, gave us the chance to sample the many ale-houses in the town. Of these it was said that their number was disproportionate to the population, but we had no complaints; as a small town it provided a great deal of social activity. I remember a party at the girls' hostel at Cloverfields and rolling a barrel of beer from the town through the snow-covered roads. The Swan hotel treated us all to Christmas dinner; there was great hospitality in the town; country dancing, and dances at Malpas (three went on a motorbike). The Railway Hotel and the Horse and Jockey in Church Street were favourite pubs.[42]

Plate 43 From Women Who Went to War *by Eric Taylor (1988), p.160, showing discarded secret wireless sets*

After leaving Whitchurch Mr. Evans went to Scotland and then to Northern Ireland.

Mr. H. Travers was sent to Whitchurch by his GPO chiefs at St. Martins-le-Grande in London. He arrived on 27 January 1947, also in a snow-storm, and it continued to snow every day for the next three months. He had been demobbed from the Navy, where he had been a wireless operator, eight or nine months previously. His billet was with Mr. and Mrs. Winterton at 13, St. John's Street. He recalls listening to government messages in code and using undulators with a tape which fed into a bin at about 100 to 200 words per minute. Next door they typed the tapes to either Bletchley Park or Eastcote by mentally translating the Morse code into 5-unit code and typing it through a guide on the teleprinter. He left in 1950.[43]

The Old Rectory was vacated and offered back to the owner, Mrs. Dentith and her family, but they were living happily elsewhere and had no desire to return. The subsequent fate of the house is reported in Chapter Six.

Appendix
(LRO, B/C/11, 3rd March 1683/4, Matthew Fowler, Rector of Whitchurch)

A true and perfect Inventory of the severall goods and Chatells of Matthew Fowler Dr in Divinity and late Rector of the p[ar]ish of Whitchurch in the County of Salop and diocesse of Lichfeild and Coventry exhibited and given in to the said Court by Lettice Fowler the Relict and executrix of the said Matthew Fowler and appraised by John Wicksteed and John Burgis two of the Inhabitants of the said Towne of Whitchurch as followeth:

Impri[m]is The bedd furniture and Chaires in the Chamber over the lower parlour	7: 10: 0
the bedd in the Stairecase Chamber	1: 0: 0
the bedd and furniture in the Chamber over the Hall . . .	4: 0: 0
the bedd in the Maids Chamber	1: 0: 0
the bedd and furniture over the little parlour	5: 10: 0
the furniture and other things in the passage Roome . . .	2: 10: 0
the bedd in Mr Wards Chamber	1: 10: 0
Lynnen	8: 0: 0
A paire of Harpsnalls	2: 10: 0
A Cup board and a table with a little Cabinet in the little parlour with Chaires	2: 0: 0
two tables in the great parlour with Chayres and stooles . .	2: 0: 0
plate	30: 0: 0
A Cabinet and Chest	3: 0: 0
All the pewter and other things in the kitchin. . . .	9: 10: 0
4 horses with Coach and harnesse	35: 0: 0
Corne and Hay	33: 0: 0
Cow and Bullocks	7: 0: 0
two tables in the Hall	3: 0: 0
Bookes	20: 0: 0
Brewing vessels barrels	3: 0: 0
Carpetts	0: 15: 0
Bills bonds and debts	700: 0: 0
utensils for husbandry	4: 0: 0
	831: 15: 0

Glossary

Apsed end: The semicircular termination of a room

Balusters: Vertical supports for the handrail of a staircase

Bay: The area between two main partitions of a building, used as a unit of measurement, e.g. 'two-bay hall'

Canted bay: Bay window which has a straight front and angled sides

Coping stone: Stone used to cap or cover a wall; flat or sloping

Cornice: The uppermost member of the entablature, projecting above the frieze. The moulding running round a room at the junction of the walls and ceiling

Cyma Recta moulding: An S-shaped moulding with the concave part uppermost

Cyma Reversa moulding: As above but with the convex part uppermost

Doric order: One of the accepted classical modes for columns with decorative heads

Eared surround: The surround of a door or window where extensions at the head resemble squared ears; sometimes 'lugged'. Popular in 18th-century work

Entablature: In classical architecture the superstructure of an Order, consisting of architrave, frieze and cornice

Flemish bond: In brickwork where alternate headers and stretchers appear in each course

Glebe land: Land belonging to the incumbent of a parish church

Hall: The traditional term for the main living-room of a house

Keystone: The central stone or brick of an arch

King Post: An upright timber standing in the centre of a tie-beam and rising to the apex of the roof

Kneeler:	A short coping-stone set horizontally at the foot of a gable slope to stop the coping stones on the slope from slipping down. Sometimes decorative
Lintel:	Horizontal beam or stone over a window, door or fireplace
Newel:	The principal post at the foot of a staircase. Sometimes the balusters curve round it
Pediment:	A low-pitched gable above a portico
Perch:	An old measurement of 16½ feet
Rood:	An old measurement of ¼ acre
Soffit:	The underside of a surface
String:	The sloping timber of a staircase holding the ends of treads and risers and supporting the balusters. Later staircases dispensed with the string and seated the balusters directly on the treads
Tie-beam:	The main transverse beam connecting opposite walls at wall-plate level
Voussoir:	A wedge-shaped stone or brick forming part of an arch

References

Abbreviations used

Cal. Pat.	Calendar of the Patent Rolls (H.M. Stationery Office, 1891–)
DNB	Dictionary of National Biography (1885–).
Eyton	R.W. Eyton, *Antiquities of Shropshire* (12 vols. 1854–60).
GCHQ	Government Communications Headquarters.
LRO	Lichfield Record Office.
Oxf. DNB	Oxford *Dictionary of National Biography* (2004).
RB	Rector's Book.
SA	Shropshire Archives, Shrewsbury.
SAS	Shropshire Archaeological and Historical Society.
SCC	Shropshire County Council.
SPR	Shropshire Parish Registers (Shropshire Parish Register Society, incorporated in SAS), followed by abbreviated name of diocese and volume no.
TSAS	*Transactions of the Shropshire Archaeological and Historical Society.*
UPSO	Universal Publishing Solutions Online.
VA	*Vernacular Architecture* (journal of the Vernacular Architecture Group).
VCH	Victoria County Histories, followed by county name and volume no.
WAAG	Whitchurch Area Archaeology Group.

Chapter 1

1. E. Ekwall, *The Concise Oxford Dictionary of English Place-Names* (4th edn. 1960), pp. 6, 146--7, 160, 241, 474; VCH Shropshire, I, 327, 331; J. Morris (gen. ed.), Domesday Book (Shropshire) (Phillimore, 1986), 4, 13, 1.
2. T.C. Duggan, *A History of Whitchurch* (1935), p. 54.
3. VCH *Shropshire*, I, p. 405.
4. P. Stamper, *The Old Rectory, Whitchurch: A Brief Site History* (SCC Archaeology Service Report No. 94, 1966), p. 1.
5. H. le Strange, *Le Strange Records 1100–1310* (London, 1916), pp. 297–8; Calendar of Inquisitions post mortem (H.M. Stationery Office 1910), pp. 309–10.
6. *Ibid.* p. 301 (citing Cal. Pat. 1321–4, p. 175).
7. Eyton, X, pp. 26–7.
8. F.B.G. Bumpus, 'Society, Government and Power in the Lordship of Blakemere, North Shropshire, *c.*1350–*c.*1420' (Univ. Coll. of Wales, Aberystwyth, Ph.D thesis, 1998), p. 33 (copy in SA, qH42).
9. Taxatio Ecclesiastica *c.*A.D. 1291, ed. T. Astle *et al.* (Record Commission, 1802), p. 247; Valor Ecclesiasticus temp. Hen. VIII, ed. J. Caley and J. Hunter (Record Commission), III (1817), p. 185.
10. Possibly a reference to a field-name featuring willows: H.D.G. Foxall, *Shropshire Field-Names* (S.A.S. 1980), p. 48; T.C. Duggan, *The Parish Church of Whitchurch* (1923), p. 36.
11. Eyton, X, p. 27; B. Ross, *Accounts of the Stewards of the Talbot Household at Blakemere 1392–1425* (Shropshire Record Series VII, 2003), p. 110.
12. B. Ross, *op. cit.* pp. 38-9, 41, 53-4, 55-6.
13. SA 3232/4. A pond ('stew') of the rector is mentioned in 1337: Cal. Pat. 1334--8, p. 556. We are grateful to Dr. F.B.G. Bumpus and Mr. G.C. Baugh for this ref. and to Mr. D. Biggins for his observation of the vivary.

Chapter 2

1. S. Watts (ed.), *The Glebe Terriers of Shropshire*, II (Shropshire Record Series VI, 2002), p. 163; L.R.O., B/V/6, Whitchurch 1612–1849.
2. We are grateful to Mrs. Nancy Cox for this info.
3. The painting was done in 1974 and is based on a photograph taken at the time. It is owned by Mr. Tom Biggins of Westry Roberts, and we are grateful to him for access to the site and for permission to photograph the painting.
4. Hearth Tax Return 1662 (copy in SA, microfilm 84).
5. Perhaps 'North Gate'.
6. RB I, 108, terrier 20 Apr. 1669.
7. M. Moran, *Vernacular Buildings of Whitchurch & Area and their Occupants* (Logaston Press, 1999), pp. 75--88; VA, XXVIII (1997), pp. 168, 170.
8. RB I, 7, 9, 11, 13, 14.

Chapter 3

1. LRO, B/C/5; RB I, 14.
2. LRO, B/V/6, Whitchurch 1612–1849; S. Watts, *op. cit.* p. 167.
3. RB I, 282a.
4. H. Colvin, *A Biographical Dictionary of British Architects 1600–1840* (J. Murray, 1978), p. 844.
5. RB I, 16, 17, 18.
6. SA 3244/1--3.
7. J. Curl, *English Architecture* (David & Charles, 1977), p. 160.
8. Pers. comm. Graham Moss.
9. J. Ionides, *Thomas Farnolls Pritchard of Shrewsbury, Architect and Inventor of Cast-Iron Bridges* (Dog Rose Press, 1999), pp. 135–6, 261–265 and passim.
10. SA, P303/F/2/3/26/1–2.

Chapter 4

1. DNB XVII (1899), pp. 154–5; J. Foster, *Alumni Oxonienses 1715–1866*, p. 415. We are grateful to Christopher Date of the British Museum for help with the land and MSS research.
2. D.H.S. Cranage, *An Architectural Account of the Churches of Shropshire*, part 8 (1906), p. 730.
3. T.C. Duggan, *The Parish Church of Whitchurch* (1923), p. 38; Shropshire County Library, *Catalogue of Books from Parochial Libraries in Shropshire* (Mansell, 1971), intro. by T. Kelly, pp. viii–ix. The library is currently held in Shropshire Archives.
4. P. Stamper, *op. cit.* p. 5; Oxf. DNB (K. Goodway on William Emes, 1729/30–1803); M. Waterson, *The Servants' Hall* (Pantheon Books, 1980), passim; A. Tinniswood, *Belton House Handbook* (Nat. Trust, 2002), p. 86.
5. RB I, 61; P. Stamper, *op. cit.* p. 6.
6. RB I, 143.
7. Ovid, *Metamorphoses*, book 2, lines 231–2.
8. Copies of the lithograph were produced and distributed, but they are very rare. For access to the one which J. North has traced we are indebted to Mary Perry. The hand-written inscription has not been included on the tracing. See M. Tonkin, 'Rector of Whitchurch who had Five Illegitimate Children', *Shropshire Magazine*, Feb. 1963, pp. 4–15; Catalogue of an Exhibition of a Selection from the Tonkin Collection Oct. 22nd –Nov. 10th 1959, no. 93 (copy in SA, D 74 v.f.; accession 9509/2); J. North, 'Which House Could it Be?', WAAG Newsletter, no. 66 (Aug. 1977), pp. 6–8.
9. RB II, 266a.
10. RB II, 262a.
11. D. Earnshaw, 'William Henry Egerton, M.A. 1811--1910', WAAG Newsletter, no. 24 (Oct. 1983), p. 5.
12. *Salopian Journal*, 5th Aug. 1795, p. 4. We are grateful to Mr Peter Criddle for this reference.
13. T.C. Duggan, *History of Whitchurch* (1935), p. 88.
14. RB I, 20, 45, 47, 49.
15. B. Falk, *The Bridgwater Millions: a candid family history* (Hutchinson, 1942), p. 187 (copy in SA, accession 1294/2); M. Tonkin, *op. cit.* p. 187.
16. B. Falk, *op. cit.* 188.
17. Transcript of Archdeacon Woodhouse's Visitations 1799–1807, pp. 39, 40, notes 5, 6, 7 (copy in SA, 3916/1/1).
18. LRO, B/A/11/2/3, p. 108.
19. RB II, 223.
20. RB II, 193.
21. RB II, 258.
22. SA 6001/2793 (Geo. Morris's 'Shropshire Genealogies', Vol. VI), p. 10.
23. *Ibid.*
24. RB I, 141.
25. RB I, 42.
26. RB II, 240--1; S. Watts, op. cit. p. 167.
27. DNB.
28. RB I, 31, 33, 35, 37; H. Colvin, op. cit. pp. 682--3.
29. RB I, 41.

Chapter Five

1. RB I, 37; H. Colvin, *op. cit*. p. 683.
2. RB I, 20.
3. LRO, B/V/6, Whitchurch 9 Sept. 1841; S. Watts, *op. cit*. p.165.
4. S. Watts, op. cit. p. 167; RB II, 238; H. Colvin, *op. cit*. pp. 405--7.
5. D.H.S. Cranage, *An Architectural Account of the Churches of Shropshire*, part 8 (1906), pp. 737–8.
6. D. Earnshaw, *op. cit*. pp. 3–6; *Whitchurch Herald*, 25 Jan. 1896, p. 5.
7. RB II, 282a; S. Watts, *op. cit*. p. 167.
8. H. Colvin, *op. cit*. pp. 128--132, 189–196; S. Parissien, *Palladian Style* (Phaidon reprint, 2000), p. 129. Shropshire houses such as Attingham Hall, Mawley Hall, Davenport House, etc., depict the Palladian influence, and apsed ends occur at Willey Hall, Hopton Court, Attingham Hall, Mawley Hall, etc. For discussion on Palladianism in Shropshire see E. Mercer, *English Architecture to 1900: The Shropshire Experience* (Logaston Press, 2003), pp. 185–8.
9. H. Colvin, *op. cit*. p. 683.
10. *Ibid*.
11. H. Colvin, *op. cit*. pp. 651--2, 829.
12. J. Ionides, *Thomas Farnolls Pritchard of Shrewsbury, Architect and 'Inventor of Cast Iron Bridges'* (Dog Rose Press, 1999).
13. M. Moran, *Vernacular Buildings of Whitchurch & Area and their Occupants* (Logaston Press, 1999), 129–138.
14. J. Ionides, *op. cit*. pp. 68, 136 and n. 26.
15. *Ibid*. pp. 88, 120, 128--129, 134; see also J. Ionides and P. Howell, *The Old Houses of Shropshire in the 19th Century: The watercolour albums of Frances Stackhouse Acton* (Dog Rose Press, 2006), pp. 82, 84.
16. J. Ionides, *T.F. Pritchard*, pp. 147--151, Facsimile, A1A15, 18, 38, 65, 78, *et al*.
17. M. Moran, *op. cit*. pp. 134--5.

Chapter Six

1. SA 2794, box 8; S. Watts, *op. cit*. p. 16.
2. M. Moran and J. Barton, *Dearnford Hall* (Logaston Press, 2003), pp. 35–6. We are grateful to Mrs. M. O'Neill for allowing us to photograph Highfields. The architect remains unknown.
3. SA 2794, Box 8.
4. *Ibid*.
5. *Ibid*.
6. *Whitchurch Herald*, 1 March 1923, sale advertisement.
7. Fulgoni's café and bakery was at 36–38 High Street. For an architectural account of this property see M. Moran, *Vernacular Buildings of Whitchurch & Area and their Occupants* (Logaston Press, 1999), pp. 101–2.
8. *Daily Telegraph*, 8 June 2000. We are grateful to Mary Le Quesne for this ref.
9. SA 2794/27, sale particulars and enclosure.
10. *Whitchurch Herald*, 4 Jan. 1935.

Chapter Seven

1. *Place-Names of Shropshire,* i (Eng. Place-Name Soc. LXII-LXIII, 1990), pp. 310–11.
2. For the descent of the manor, etc., see Eyton, X, pp. 14–25; J.H. Round, *Family Origins and other Studies*, ed. W. Page (1930), pp. 48–50; F.B.G. Bumpus, 'Society, Government and Power in the Lordship of Blakemere *c.*1350–*c.*1420' (Univ. of Wales, Aberystwyth, Ph.D. thesis, 1998), pp. 33–6; VCH *Shropshire*, III, p. 310; IV, p. 133; G.E. C[okayne], *Complete Peerage*, II, pp. 311–16, 349–50; XI, pp. 698–716; XII (1), pp. 341–6, 616–20; Burke, *Peerage* (1999), pp. 395–7.
3. Cf. Lichfield Diocesan Directory 1988/9, p. 83; 1989/90, p. 85.
4. *Taxatio Ecclesiastica c.A.D. 1291*, ed. T. Astle *et al*. (Record Commission, 1802), p. 247; *Accounts of the Stewards of the Talbot Household at Blakemere 1392–1425*, ed. B. Ross (Shropshire Record Series, VII, 2003), pp. 38–9, 53–4, 182.
5. *Taxatio Ecclesiastica*, pp. 157–76, 241–65, 285–90. Precise comparisons for 1291 are impeded by the difficulty of distinguishing between appropriated and unappropriated rectories as recorded in the *Taxatio*.
6. *Valor Ecclesiasticus temp. Hen. VIII*, ed. J. Caley and J. Hunter (Record Commission), III (1817), p. 185.
7. *Ibid*. pp. 189–99, 200–5, 208–16; IV (1821), pp. 448–9. Next in value was Edgmond, worth £48.
8. The 1535 figures notwithstanding, Edgmond was probably always the richer living, as the Provost's House (the Rectory until 1926) helps to show: see E. Mercer, *English Architecture to 1900: The Shropshire Experience* (Logaston Press, 2003), pp. 110–11; N. Pevsner, *Shropshire* (The Buildings of England), pp. 125–6.
9. *Rep. Com. Eccl. Revenues* [67], pp. 506--7, H.C. (1835), XXII.
10. The richer livings were Stone (Staffs.) £3,000, Edgmond £2,900, Hodnet £2,336, Wem £2,250, and Aston-juxta-Birmingham (Warws.) £2,082: *ibid*. pp. 98–109, 428–509.

11. LRO, B/V/6, Whitchurch 1845 and 1849, record 29½ a. and 35 a. respectively. The 1887 figure is likely to be more accurate.
12. Return of Glebe Land 1887, H.C. 307, p. 68 (1887), LXIV.
13. Crockford's *Clerical Directory* 1938, 556; 1939, 558; 1941, preface p. xi.
14. Private information.
15. Cal. Pat. 1292–1301, p. 276.
16. Eyton, X, p. 27; LRO, B/A/1/1, f. 65–65v.; B/A/1/2, f. 214v. For Bevis de Knovill see above; VCH *Shropshire*, III, p. 17; Sir M. Powicke, *The Thirteenth Cent. 1216–1307* (1970), pp. 414–15; J.B. Blakeway, *The Sheriffs of Shropshire* (Shrewsbury, 1831), pp. 8, 46.
17. Cal. Pat. 1334–8, p. 556; LRO, B/A/1/2, ff. 214v., 232v.
18. Eyton, X, p. 27; LRO, B/A/1/2, f. 232v.
19. Eyton, X, pp. 27, 368–9, 376.
20. Cal. Pat. 1367–70, p. 83; Lichfield R.O., B/A/1/6, f. 3. The king was patron during the minority of the heir of his late tenant in chief John, Lord Strange of Blakemere (d.1361). Ludlow may possibly have been a member of the family which, prospering mightily in the 13th-cent. wool trade, bought Stokesay and married the heiress of Hodnet, thus making their way into county society: VCH *Shropshire*, IV, p. 60; Eyton, V, pp. 36, 290; IX, pp. 333–6.
21. Eyton, X, p. 27; LRO, B/A/1/6, ff. 68v.–69.
22. Eyton, X, p. 27; LRO, B/A/1/7, ff. 115v., 147, 149v.; see above, this chapter and chapter 1, for the letting of the living.
23. Eyton, X, p. 27; LRO, B/A/1/7 f. 115v.
24. SA 212/19/3, ff. 1, 2; /19/5, f. 1 (cited in Bumpus, 'Lordship of Blakemere', pp. 106--7).
25. LRO, B/A/1/9. ff. 96, 97v.; A. B. Emden, Biographical Register of the University of Oxford to 1500 (1957–9), III, pp. 2120–1, which does not, however, mention the rectory of Whitchurch. The patron had been at Windsor with the infant king Hen. VI in the autumn of 1422 (G.E.C. *Complete Peerage*, XI, p. 700) and had possibly come across this civil servant there.
26. LRO, B/A/1/9, f. 97v. For his career see Emden, *Biog. Reg. Oxf.* II, p. 929.
27. LRO, B/A/1/9, f. 106. Cf. Emden, *Biog. Reg. Oxf.* I, p. 473; A.B. Emden, *Biographical Register of the University of Cambridge* (1963), p. 153.
28. LRO, B/A/1/9, f. 106; *ibid.* /11, f. 34v. For Talbot see Oxf. DNB; his will is printed in TSAS, 3rd ser. IV, pp. 371–8.
29. LRO, B/A/1/11, ff. 34v., 35v., 43v.; *ibid.* /12, f. 92; Emden, *Biog. Reg. Oxf.* III, p. 1825.
30. LRO, B/A/1/12, ff. 92, 95; *ibid.* /13, f. 155. The king presented by reason of the minority of the patron, George Talbot, 4th Earl of Shrewsbury, and the earl, having meanwhile come of age, presented Talbot in 1489, when he had to be instituted to Whitchurch again after having accepted other, incompatible, preferment.
31. LRO, B/A/1/13, ff. 155, 228; Emden, *Biog. Reg. Oxf.* III, p. 1685.
32. LRO, B/A/1/13, f. 228; /14(iii), f. 31; Emden, *Biog. Reg. Oxf.* III, p. 1946.
33. LRO, B/A/1/14(iii), f. 31. See Emden, Biog. Reg. Oxf. III, pp. 1844–5; VCH *Shropshire*, II, p. 159.
34. TSAS, 3rd ser. I, p. 259.
35. *Ibid.* p. 260.
36. *Ibid.* p. 261; J. Foster, *Alumni Oxonienses 1500–1714* (1891–2), II, p. 591.
37. TSAS, 3rd ser. V, p. 350; Foster, *Alum. Oxon. 1500–1714*, IV, p. 1359; J. and J.A. Venn, *Alumni Cantabrigienses* (1922–54): to 1751, IV, p. 81; *The History of the University of Oxford*, IV (Seventeenth-Century Oxford), ed. N. Tyacke (1997), pp. 184, 574–5.
38. LRO, B/V/6, Whitchurch 1612.
39. LRO, B/A/1/16, ff. 83v.–84; TSAS, 3rd ser. I, p. 264; Foster, *Alum. Oxon. 1500–1714*, III, p. 1236; *Hist. Univ. of Oxf.* IV, ed. Tyacke, p. 188; H. Trevor-Roper, *Archbishop Laud 1573–1645* (1988), pp. 42–3; S.A., P303/A/1/1, bur. 10 Feb. 1630/1.
40. LRO, B/A/1/16, ff. 83v.–84; TSAS, 3rd ser. I, p. 264; V, p. 353; VII, pp. 252, 254, 260, 288; LXXIII, p. 40; Foster, *Alum. Oxon. 1500–1714*, II, p. 525. For the Fowler fam. see VCH *Staffordshire*, XX, p. 23.
41. See below. For the brothers see G.H.F. Vane, 'On Two Rectors of Whitchurch', TSAS, 2nd ser. XII. 283–98.
42. TSAS, 2nd ser. XII, pp. 284–5; 3rd ser. VII, pp. 254, 258, 260, 267, 271, 284, 295–6, 305–6; LXXIII, pp. 34, 36–7, 40, 41; Venn, *Alum. Cantab. to 1751*, III, p. 382; *The People of God: Shrews. Dissenters 1660–1699*, ed. J.V. Cox (Shropshire Record Series, IX, 2006), pp. xlvii, lii, lv, lviii, lxix. For the 2nd Earl of Bridgwater see Oxf. DNB.
43. Cromwell at Sidney Sussex College: Oxf. DNB.
44. Oxf. DNB.; LRO, B/A/1/17, p. 2.
45. Clavi trabales; or, Nailes fastned by some great Masters of Assemblyes Confirming the Kings supremacy, The subjects duty, Church government by bishops (1661; preface by Rob. Sanderson, Bp. of Lincoln).
46. SA, P303/A/1/3, bur. 7 Nov. 1661.
47. LRO, B/A/1/17, p. 2; TSAS, 4th ser. IV, p. 181; Foster, *Alum. Oxon. 1500–1714*, II, p. 701.
48. T.S.A.S. 2nd ser. XII, pp. 285–98; 3rd ser. I, pp. 152, 373; 4th ser. IV, p. 186; Foster, *Alum. Oxon. 1500–1714*, II, p. 525.
49. Venn, *Alum. Cantab. to 1751*, IV, p. 20.

50. TSAS, 4th ser. V, p. 187; G. Ormerod, *Hist. Co. Palatine of Chester* (1883), I, pp. 433, 446, 455–6; Foster, *Alum. Oxon. 1500–1714*, III, p. 898; S.P.R. Lich. XIX (1), pp. vii, ix; Venn, *Alumni Cantab. to 1751*, III, pp. 62, 63.

51. S.P.R. Lich. XIX (1), p. ix; Burke, *Peerage* (1967), p. 2022; VCH *Staffordshire*, III, p. 68.

52. TSAS, 4th ser. V, p. 199; Venn, *Alum. Cantab. to 1751*, III, p. 247; N.L.W., SA/MB/46; V.C.H. Mdx. X, pp. 161–2; *The Parish of St. Anne Soho* (Survey of London XXXIII–XXXIV, 1966), pp. 213–14; for Peter Newcome see Oxf. DNB.

53. TSAS, 4th ser. V, p. 206; Foster, *Alum. Oxon. 1715–1886* (1887–8), II, p. 415.

54. TSAS, 4th ser. VI, p. 296.

55. *Ibid.* p. 297; SPR Lich. XIX (1), p. ix; Oxf. D.N.B.

56. Foster, *Alum. Oxon. 1715–1886*, IV, p. 1389; Oxf. DNB.; *The History of the University of Oxford*, V (The Eighteenth Century), ed. L.S. Sutherland and L.G. Mitchell (1986), pp. 421–2, 621–2, 625, 628–32, 635; VI (Nineteenth-Century Oxford Part I), ed. M.G. Brock and M.C. Curthoys (1997), pp. xii, 9, 13, 292, 341 and Plate 5.

57. Burke, *Land. Gent.* (1952), p. 1563; Burke, *Peerage* (1967), p. 1455; J M. Wilson, *Imperial Gazetteer of Eng. and Wales* (1870–2); J. and J.A. Venn, *Alumni Cantabrigienses* (1922–54): 1752–1900, IV, p. 204.

58. G. Ormerod, *Hist. Co. Palatine of Chester* (1883), II, pp. 222–3, 301, 629; Burke, *Peerage* (1967), p. 854; Burke, *Land. Gent.* (1952), p. 769; SPR Lich. XIX (1), p. ix; for the Ethelstons see A.A.P. Ethelston, 'The Ethelston Fam. and Hinton Hall', WAAG Newsletter, no. 45 (Aug. 1990), pp. 5–6.

59. Crockford's *Clerical Dir.* 1910, p. 430.

60. For the Dugdales see Burke, *Land. Gent.* (18th edn.), I (1965), p. 218.

61. Possibly embellished by T.F. Pritchard; demolished in 1975: R. Haslam, *Powys* (Bldgs. of Wales, 1979), p. 134.

62. Kelly's *Dir. Salop.* (1895–1929); VCH *Shropshire*, III, p. 192.

63. Kelly's *Dir. Salop.* (1895–1929).

64. Burke, *Land. Gent.* (1937), p. 767.

65. *Who Was Who 1951–60* (1961), p. 483.

66. Crockford's *Clerical Dir.* 1920, p. 437; Suppl. 1942–44, p. 53; Kelly's *Dir. Salop.* (1941), p. 333.

67. Burke, *Peerage* (1967), p. 1159; Burke, *Land. Gent.* (1952), p. 769; Venn, *Alum. Cantab. 1752–1900*, III, p. 227; Crockford's *Clerical Dir.* 1920, p. 647.

68. Crockford's *Clerical Dir.* 1930, p. 527; Venn, *Alum. Cantab. 1752–1900*, III, p. 154.

69. Crockford's *Clerical Dir.* 1938, 556; 1965-6, 505.

70. Crockford's *Clerical Dir.* 1965–6, pp. 204–5, 1761.

71. Crockford's *Clerical Dir.* 1973–4, pp. 500, 1249; *Lichfield Diocesan Directory* 1997/8, p. 24.

72. Crockford's *Clerical Dir.* 2000/1, pp. 613, 1045; 2004/5, p. 665.

Chapter Eight

1. N. West, *GCHQ: The Secret of Wireless Intelligence* (Weidenfeld & Nicolson, 1986), p. 7.

2. *Ibid.*

3. *Ibid.* p. 10.

4. *Ibid.* p. 11.

5. *Ibid.* p. 15.

6. *Ibid.* pp. 21–27.

7. *Ibid.* pp. 27–31.

8. *Ibid.* p. 39.

9. *Ibid.* p. 95.

10. *Ibid.*

11. *Ibid.* pp. 96–108.

12. G. Pidgeon, *The Secret Wireless War* (UPSO, 2003), p. 328.

13. N. West, *op. cit.* p. 110.

14. *Ibid.* p. 120.

15. *Ibid.* p. 126.

16. G. Pidgeon, *op. cit.* p. xx.

17. D. White, 'Diplomatic Wireless Service at Bletchley Park' (pers. comm. to S. North dated 3 Feb. 1998).

18. SA 3244/1/2/3. That dated 24 Oct. 1941 is BMV 62/R2. That dated May 1942 and numbered 28 is a site plan labelled 'PO Reserve Station Old Rectory Whitchurch'. Produced by the Sanitary Engineering Branch, Birmingham, it labels the farm building block with its yards, stables, the main drive to the main road and the new by-pass.

19. D. White, pers. comm. (*ut supra*).

20. H. Mahmud, pers. comm. 2 Mar. 2005; Radio Society of Great Britain, pers. comm. 22 Mar. 2005.

21. Mrs. B. Hayes, pers. comm., interview, 4 Oct. 2002.

22. F.H. Hinslip and A. Stripp, *Codebreakers: The Inside Story of Bletchley Park* (Oxf. Univ. Press, 1994), p. 132.
23. As note 21.
24. R. Denniston, *Churchill's Secret War* (Sutton Publishing, 1997), Appendix 2.
25. *Ibid.* pp. xii, 11, 19.
26. As note 21.
27. Mrs. J. Briggs, pers. comm. 6 May 2004.
28. Mrs. M. Rudd, pers. comm. 8 Dec. 2004
29. Mrs. J. Broadhurst, pers. comm. 2004.
30. Mrs. B. Griffiths, pers. comm. 1 Oct. 2004.
31. J. Nicholls, *The Story of Beaumanor 'Y' Station* (private publication, 1988), p. 54.
32. Mrs. B. Hayes, as note 21.
33. *Whitchurch Herald*, 11 Jan. 2001, p. 15.
34. M. Smith, *Station X* (Channel Four Books, 1998), p. 52.
35. I. Valentine, *Station 43* (Sutton Publishing Ltd., 2004), p. 100.
36. N. West, *op. cit.* p. 192.
37. Mr. Elliot Mead, pers. comm. 23 Mar. 2004.
38. Mrs. J. Broadhurst, as note 27.
39. Mrs. J. Briggs, as note 25.
40. J. Nicholls, *op. cit.* p. 139.
41. M. Smith, *op. cit.* p. 176.
42. J.D. Evans, pers. comm. 2 Feb. 2004.
43. H. Travers, pers. comm. 14 Mar. 1998.

Additional Bibliography

J. Pether, *Funkers and Sparkers* (Bletchley Park Report, 2000)
R.V. Jones, *Most Secret War* (Hodder & Stoughton, 1978)

Index

Advowson 3, 49
Austerberry, Archdeacon 59

Bamfield, Veronica 45-46
Baudot code 80
Baxter, Richard 53
Bernard, Nicholas 53-54
Blakemere 2, 3
Bletchley Park 68, 79-81
Botiller, Ankaret 3
    William 3
Brereton, Sir William 53
Briggs, June 77, 84, 85
Broadhurst, Joan 77, 83
Brook Farm, Chester Road 87
Brookes, James 52
Brownlow, Earls /Barons 49

Carr, Mr. (Jon) 23, 24, 27, 28, 39, 40
Chamberlain, Charles Arthur 60
Civil War, The 53
Cloverfields 76
Colossus 81
Cromwell, Oliver 53
Cubitt, Gen. Sir Thomas Astley 45
    Veronica (*see under* Bamfield)
Cumber, John 51

Davies, Raymond 59
de Bo(e)rdefeld(e), Bartholomew 3, 50
de Kno(u)vill, Bevis 49
    John 3, 50
de Thrisk, Roger 3, 51
(de) Warenne family 2
    Alianore 2
    William, Earls 2, 49
Dentith family 48
    Rev. O.A. 46-47
Dodington, chapel of St. Catherine 39
Domesday Book 1, 2
Dovaston, Nicholas 50
Dugdale, Sydney 43, 58

Egerton family 49
    Francis Henry 21-32, 55-56
        absences of 28
        Act for relief of poor of Whitchurch 26

        Bridgwater Treatises 22
        lawsuit with Mr. Wickstead 25-26
        library 22-23
        manuscripts 22
        pets, and 28
        school administration 28-29
        Workhouse, and 26
    'General' 20
    Hon Henry 55
    Henry 55
    Sir Thomas 49
    William Henry 39. 40. 42, 57-58
Emes, William 23
Enigma machines 65-67, 80
Ethelfleda, lady of the Mercians 1
Evans, Mr. J.D. 87

Fowler, Matthew 5, 54
    Thomas 53
Fraunceys, James 3, 50

Green End House 43
Griffith, William Charles 59
Griffiths, Betty 77, 84
Grossett, Lt. 'Jack' 82

Halifax, James 55
Hall, John Henry 50, 60
Hanmer, Hugh 43, 44, 59
    Richard 44, 45, 46
Hayes, Betty 84, 85
Heylin, Richard 54
Heyworth, John 51
Highfields 43, 44
Hollies, The 82
Holmes, George 72-73, 75, 77
Hooper, Roger 48

Jenkins, Richard David 59, 60

Knight, Mr. 26

Latham, Sydney 59
le Strange family 2, 3, 49
    Ankaret (*see under* Talbot)
    Fulk 2, 3, 49
    John 3

Robert 2, 3, 50
Leigh, Peter 55
Long family 56-57
   Charles Maitland 33, 34, 39, 56-57
   Edward 55
   Edward Noel 56, 57
   Robert Ballard 56, 57
Ludlow, John 50

MacDonald, Capt. 46
   Joe 79
Mawdesley, Thomas 52
Mawson, Basil 59
McKay, Miss 77
Mead, Elliott (Percy) 81
Morrall, Henry 28

Newcome, Richard 11, 55
Nicolls, Joan 78
Nitzens, James 52

Porden, Charles 34-39, 41
Porter, Thomas 53
Pridding, Mrs. 47, 48
Pritchard, Thomas Farnolls 12, 41, 42

Rawlinson, John 52
Rectorama, The 60-62
Rectory 11-20
   alterations to 23-24, 30-32, 33-39
   architect, question as to 12, 19-20, 40-42
   coach-house 5-6, 42
   dog-kennel 26-27
   faculty for new 11
   gate-house 12
   Ice-house 39
   kindergarten school at 47-48
   library 22-23, 43, 45
   Old (demolished in 1749) 5-9
   sale particulars 1923 44-45
       1933 46-47
   staircase 19-20
   'Y' Station, as 63-88
      Morse, high speed 78-79
      Naval Section 81-83
Reeves, Bishop Stretton 59
Restoration, The 53
Reveley, Henry Willey 33, 38-39, 41
   Willey 24, 30-32, 38-39, 41
Richards, Henry 59
Ridley, Andrew Roy 60

Rudd, Mary 77

Sankey, Clement 6, 8, 54
Sharratt, Bill 73, 75
Shirburn, Richard 52
Singleton, Thomas 52
Smith, Robert Thursfield 43
Snowdon, Miss 87
Stankey, Thomas 50
Stanley, Richard 51
Stedeman, Roger 51
Sutton, Thomas 51

Talbot, Ankaret 3
   Christopher 52
   John, 1st Earl 3, 39-40, 51
   John 52
   Richard, Lord 49
Tatham, Edward 33
Thompson, Mr. 73, 75
Thorne, Frank 73, 75
Tilley, Tom 73, 75, 77
Tithes 29, 50
   Barn 5, 6
Travers, Mr. H. 87
Turing, Alan 80
Turner, Samuel 8, 9. 12
TypeX machines 67, 71

Ussher, Archbishop 53

Vernon, Edgar 'Teddy' 73, 75, 76, 77
   George 52
Vivary 4

Walker, Olive 47, 48
Wallace, Mr. 27
Welford, Thomas 51
Weston, Mrs. 87
Whitchurch, origins 1-2
   Minster church 2
Whitfield, Betty & Peter 83
Whitlam, Lofty 83
Wickstead, William 25-26
Williams, Bill 77
Windsor, Arthur 59
Winterton, Mr. & Mrs. 88
Woods, Tommy 73, 75, 77
Woodward, George 73, 77
Wymbysh, Nicholas 51